Spelling and Vocabulary

Vocabulary

1

Teacher's Guide

Author:
Mary Ellen Quint, Ph.D.

Editor:
Alan Christopherson, M.S.

Graphic Design:
Lauren Durain, A.S.T., Jennifer L. Davis, B.S.

Illustration:
Alpha Omega Creative Services

Alpha Omega Publications, Inc. • Rock Rapids, IA

©MMI by Alpha Omega Publications, Inc.

804 N. 2nd Ave. E., Rock Rapids, IA 51246-1759
All rights reserved.

Printed in the United States of America

ISBN 978-0-7403-0214-5

Spelling and Vocabulary 1

Teacher's Guide

Contents

Introduction

Introduction

"Whatever you do, work at it with all your heart, as working for the Lord, not for men."
(Colossians 3:23).

Approaches to spelling have changed over the years from simple rote memorization of words, often outside any context, to an integrated study of words in relation to their use in the language. Spelling programs today move in many directions. Most present some selection of words to be studied, memorized, and used in a written context. Others present guidelines for approaching spelling but leave the choice of words to the teacher, who must then determine which words the children need to know how to spell for successful completion of writing assignments and the study of individual subjects. Whatever approach is taken, most programs agree that words must be studied within the context of the language —within word families—and that words must be used in a written context.

Horizons Spelling Program Features

The Horizons Spelling Program presents words chosen from lists of most frequently-used words, sight words, and words chosen for particular phonetic or rhyming patterns. Each lesson also supplies space for two additional "Working Words" — words chosen by the teacher or parent that apply to the child's experience with words. These "Working Words" can be taken from other subject areas or chosen on an individual basis from words frequently used, but misspelled, in the child's daily writing.

The program consists of 160 lessons that can be covered in a 32-week period, an average of 5 lessons per week. This should accommodate classroom schedules for the school year. Home schooling schedules, which are more flexible, may spend more or less time, depending on the child's progress.

A *Spelling Dictionary* is provided for the spelling words. This dictionary is presented as a separate volume from the Spelling text so that the children may use it more easily and avoid having to move back and forth from the lesson to the back of the book. Space is also provided at the end of the dictionary for the "Working Words" selected for each week. Children enter their words in the dictionary each week, writing them under the appropriate letter of the alphabet.

Weekly Schedule

Day 1: Assess child's knowledge and introduce words

Day 2: Examine and explore words

Day 3: Look at context and meaning of words

Day 4: Apply understanding of words in writing

Day 5: Assess and evaluate progress

The Horizons Spelling Program provides pages for assessment within the context of the week's lessons. The first page of each new set of lessons is entitled "What Do You Know?" The last page of each set is for testing, correction, and practice.

"What Do You Know?"

This page is a simple assessment tool to see what children already know about the Words for the Week. It is **NOT** used as a **PRE-TEST**.

No grades are kept.

The Words for the Week are said aloud by the teacher, repeated in the context of a sentence, then repeated again.

1. The child writes each word as he/she thinks it is spelled on the lines in the first column.

2. When all words have been given, the teacher may choose to write the words on the board, spelling each as it is written.

3. Invite the children to compare their words with the one written on the board. For small classes or home schooling families, this word study can be done on an individual basis.

4. Answer any questions they may have, and point out any features of the word that will help them to see it in relation to other words in the list, or other words they know (rhyming patterns, same initial or final consonant, etc.)

5. Have the children fold their page over one column so that they can see the list of Words for the Week on the following page (as illustrated at right).

6. Ask the children to take a crayon or colored pencil to make their words match the spelling of the words in the list.

7. When they have done this, the teacher checks each student's list and writes the corrections for misspelled words in the **Corrections** column.

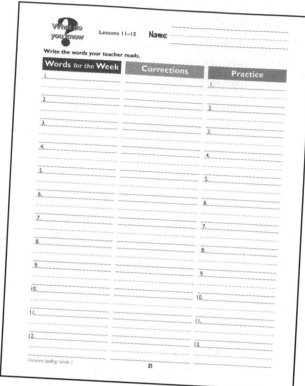

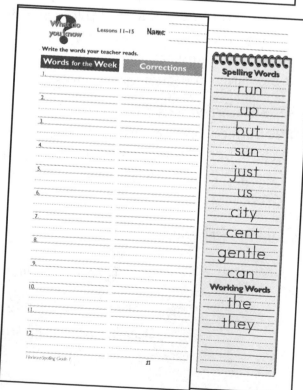

This process is extremely important. It gives the teacher an insight into the child's understanding of words and sounds. It gives the teacher an early indication of problems, such as reversals of letters. It gives the teacher an opportunity to work with the child, complimenting all efforts and correctly spelled words (or even parts of words), encouraging the child, and helping the child approach the spelling of unknown words.

8. The child then practices writing the corrected words in the **Practice** column.

9. On the second side of the page, the child has a word box containing the Words for the Week. Go over the words one by one.

10. Help the child to write two sentences using some of the Words for the Week. This may be done initially as a class project in which one sentence is written on the board for the entire class to copy, but it should move to the point where each child can write his/her own sentences.

11. Practice space is given for all the words AND for the Working Words chosen for the week.

This second page (shown below) may be used as extra in-class work, or sent home as a study guide.

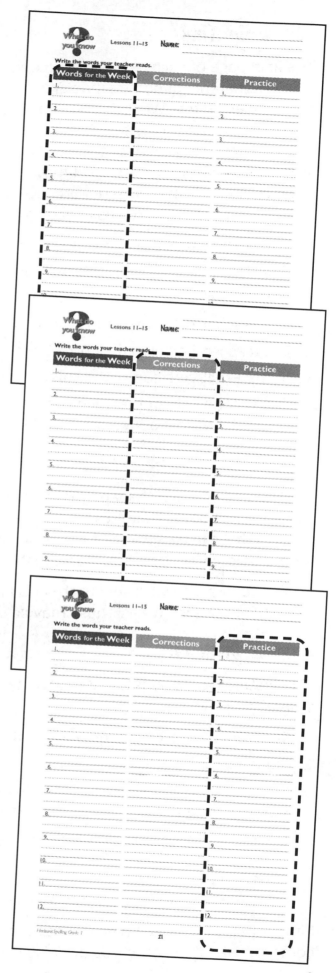

"Check-Up Time"

The final page of each week's work (Lessons 5, 10, 15, 20, 25, etc.) is an assessment page. Teachers/parents of home schoolers can decide what will be assessed. If a child did exceptionally well on the "What do you know?" pre-assessment, the teacher may choose not to test words already known by the child. The teacher may also choose to test all Words for the Week. Space is provided for the word list given, but make sure that the two "choice" Working Words for the week are tested. It may be wise to keep a notebook on each child in which you will record words that present particular difficulties. These words could be added to review lists or used to replace words already mastered in a review unit.

1. The teacher says the word, repeats it in the context of a sentence, then repeats the word.
2. The child writes the word dictated in the **Spelling Test** column.
3. The process is repeated until all words have been tested.
4. The teacher may correct in class by writing the words on the board.
5. The teacher then uses the **Corrections** column to write any corrections for words misspelled.
6. In the **Practice** column, the child copies the correct spelling of any words missed.
7. The second side of the page can be used for retesting, for testing additional sight or "Working Words" added for the week, and for additional practice.

Reproducible Teaching Aids

Spelling/phonics rules that apply to the lessons are included in the teacher's guide rather than in the student book. They are listed in the individual lessons, but are also found in reproducible masters that can be enlarged for bulletin board use, or copied to make individual "rule books" for the children. Go over the rules with the children at the beginning of each week's lesson.

Additional practice worksheets are also included as reproducible masters. There is one worksheet for each week. These may be used in class or as homework assignments.

Spelling Dictionary

The *Spelling Dictionary* is an integral part of the Horizons Spelling Program and accomplishes several purposes:

1. Students will become acquainted with the format and function of a simplified dictionary.
2. Students will be able to see and read their spelling words used in the context of a sentence.
3. Students will have an opportunity to practice their alphabetizing and reading/writing skills by using the *Spelling Dictionary* to perform the following tasks:
   - Look up the spelling words at the beginning of each week's lessons.
   - Record their weekly "Working Words" in the appropriate location at the back of the Spelling Dictionary.
   - Use the *Spelling Dictionary* as a resource for writing sentences and stories.

Simple parts of speech (verbs, nouns, and proper nouns) are identified, and plural and comparative forms of words are also shown.

Word Family Charts and Notebooks

Word families involve words that have the same phonogram. If the families are based on the ending sound the words in each family will rhyme. Some of the most common word families in English are: -ab, -ack, -ag, -ail, -ain, -ake, -ale, -all, -am, -an, -ank, -ap, -ash, -at, -ate, -aw, -ay, -eat, -ed, -eed, -ell, -est, -ew, -ice, -ick, -ide, -ight, -ill, -im, -in, -ine, -ing, -ink, -ip, -it, -ob, -ock, -oke, -op, -ore, -ot, -out, -ow, -uck, -ug, -um, -unk, -y.

Skilled readers recognize patterns in words and rather than sound out a word letter by letter will decode new words based on predictable patterns that they already know. If a student can read the word cat then it is very likely that he/she will be able to read other –at words like sat, mat, flat, pat, splat, hat, that, brat, or chat. These words all have the same chunks or rimes as the word ending.

Word families can also be based on the vowel sound, on the initial consonant sound, or on other categories of similarity. The student will get additional exposure to the words as he/she sorts and classifies them into these groups.

To extend and enhance the learning of each week's word list the teacher's notes for this course suggest that word family charts be made that can be posted in the classroom. This will be an ongoing process in which words will be added to each category as they are introduced in the course. To further extend this process, the student should compile a notebook or notebooks of word families. These notebooks can be used as a resource for the next grade level and the student can add new words to them as they are introduced.

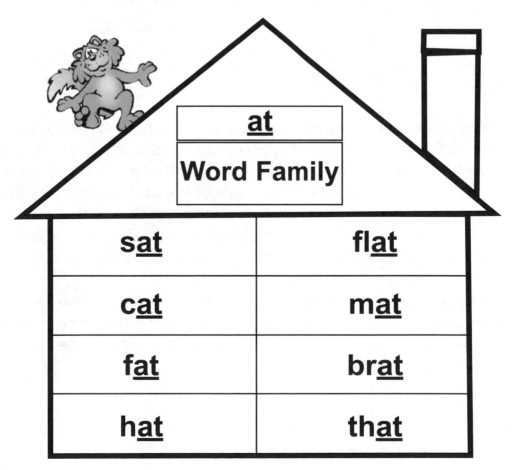

<u>at</u> Word Family	
s<u>at</u>	fl<u>at</u>
c<u>at</u>	m<u>at</u>
f<u>at</u>	br<u>at</u>
h<u>at</u>	th<u>at</u>

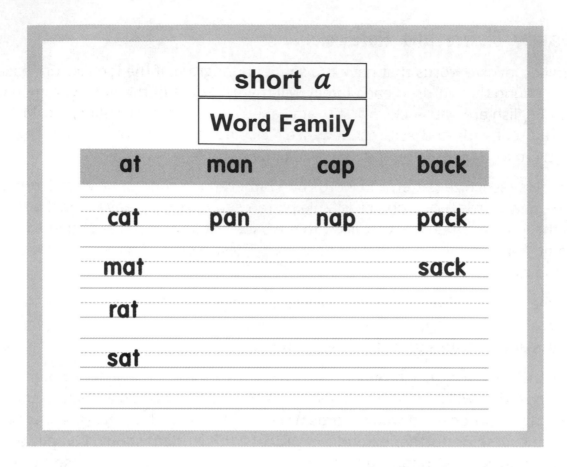

short a			
Word Family			
at	man	cap	back
cat	pan	nap	pack
mat			sack
rat			
sat			

Penmanship

The student workbooks have perforated pages so the lesson sheets can be removed from the book for the student. Removing the pages is essential to promoting good penmanship. It will be impossible for the student to write neatly on the pages if they are only folded back on the binding of the book. The raised edge of the center binding of the book will prohibit the student's hand from holding a consistent position as they write across the page. After the lesson pages have been completed, they can be punched and stored in a 3-ring binder. Completed lessons can be used for drill, review, and preparation for the test.

Although this course is not a formal penmanship program, guidelines have been provided on all of the student pages to promote good penmanship. A letter formation guide is provided in both the Teacher's Guide and the Student Workbook. This guide can be followed or if you wish, another style can be used.

Correct Formation of Manuscript Letters and Numbers

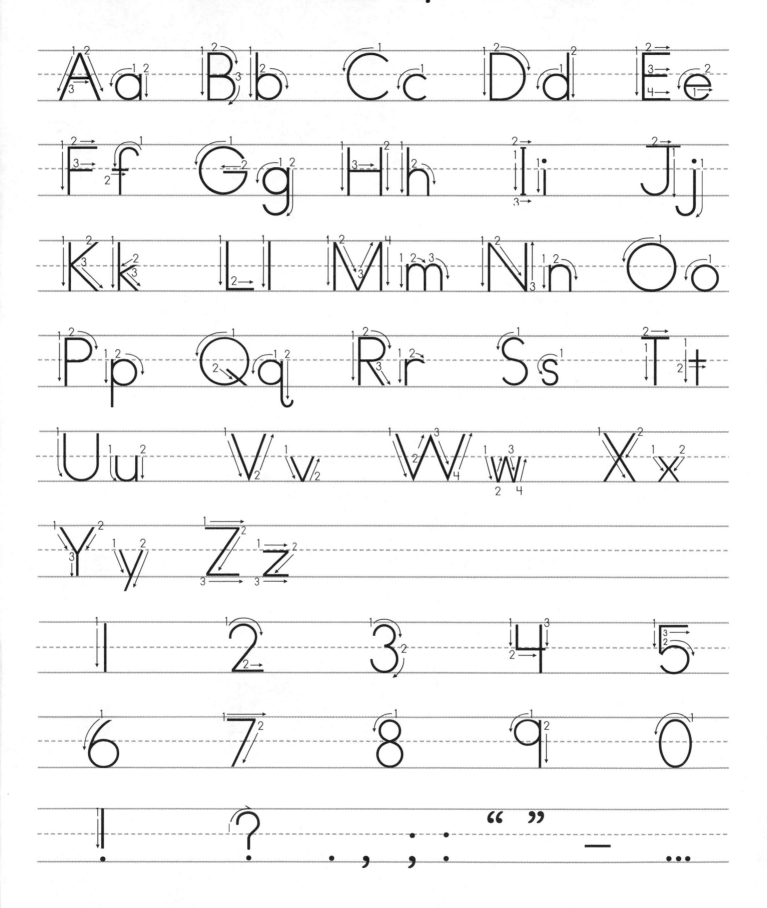

Scope & Sequence

Week 1

Lessons 1-5:

Goal: To recognize and spell short ă and short ĕ words.

Week 2

Lessons 6-10:

Goal: To recognize and spell short ĭ and short ŏ words.

Week 3

Lessons 11-15:

Goal: To recognize and spell short ŭ words and words with hard and soft **c** and **g**.

Week 4

Lessons 16-20:

Goal: To recognize and spell words with the long ā sound.

Week 5

Lessons 21-25:

Goal: To recognize and spell words with the long ē sound.

Week 6

Lessons 26-30:

Goal: To recognize and spell words with the long ī sound.

Week 7

Lessons 31-35:

Goal: To recognize and spell words with the long ō sound.

Week 8

Lessons 36-40:

Goal: Review words and patterns from Lessons 1–35.

Week 9

Lessons 41-45:

Goal: To recognize and spell words with the long ū sound, and with the /ks/ sound of **x**.

Week 10

Lessons 46-50:

Goals: To recognize, spell, and understand contractions; to spell words ending in double letters.

Week 11

Lessons 51-55:

Goal: To recognize and spell plural words ending in –**s** and –**es**.

Week 12

Lessons 56-60:

Goal: To recognize and spell words used in comparisons ending with the suffixes –**er** and –**est**.

Week 13

Lessons 61-65:

Goal: To recognize and learn to spell words with the suffixes **–ful**, **–ing**, and **–ness**.

Week 14

Lessons 66-70:

Goals: To recognize and spell words with silent letters: **igh**, **mb**, **ck**, **kn**, **gn**, **gn**, **wr**, and **wh**; to spell two common abbreviated words.

Week 15

Lessons 71-75:

Goal: To recognize and spell words with the long and short **oo** sound and the three sounds of **ea**.

Week 16

Lessons 76-80:

Goal: To review words from Lessons 41–75.

Week 17

Lessons 81-85:

Goal: To recognize and spell words with **ou**, **ow**, **au**, and **aw**.

Week 18

Lessons 86-90:

Goal: To recognize and spell words with **oi**, **oy**, and compound words.

Week 19

Lessons 91-95:

Goal: To recognize and spell words with **l** and **r** consonant blends.

Week 20

Lessons 96-100:

Goal: To recognize and spell words with beginning **s** blends: **st**, **sl**, **sm**, **sn**, **sk**, and **sp**.

Week 21

Lessons 101-105:

Goal: To recognize and spell words beginning with **sh**, and **th**.

Week 22

Lessons 106-110:

Goal: To recognize and spell words with the **ch** and **ck** wounds.

Week 23

Lessons 111-115:

Goal: To recognize and spell words beginning with **wh** and words ending in **tch**.

Week 24

Lessons 116-120:

Goal: To review spelling words from Lessons 81–115.

Week 25

Lessons 121-125:

Goal: To recognize and spell words that are **synonyms**.

Week 26

Lessons 126-130:

Goal: To recognize and spell words that are **antonyms**.

Week 27

Lessons 131-135:

Goal: To recognize and spell words that are **homophones**.

Week 28

Lessons 136-140:

Goal: To recognize and spell **ar** and **or** words.

Week 29

Lessons 141-145:

Goal: To recognize and spell **ir**, **er**, and **ur** words.

Week 30

Lessons 146-150:

Goal: To recognize and spell words with these sounds: **qu**, **ph**, **gh**, **igh**, and **ould**.

Week 31

Lessons 151-155:

Goal: To recognize and spell words with the **al** sound and words ending in –**ed** and –**ing**.

Week 32

Lessons 156-160:

Goal: To review spelling words from Lessons 117–155.

Teacher Lessons

Week 1

Lessons 1-5: Assess Child's Knowledge

Goal: To recognize and spell short ă and short ĕ words. (See the **Reproducible Phonics Rules Flashcards** at the end of this Teacher's Guide.)

1. **Short Vowel Rule:** When a word or syllable has only one vowel and it comes between two consonants, or at the beginning of the word or syllable, the vowel is usually short.
   Examples: **at**, **man**, **pan**, **hen**, **get**.

2. Review the short vowel sign (˘) with the children.

3. Review rules:
   Vowels: a, e, i, o u, and sometimes y.

   Consonants: all the other letters of the alphabet and, usually, y.

4. Point out the word "**I**" and tell the students that it always is spelled with a capital letter.

What Do You Know?

Give the students the What do you know? page for Lessons 1-5 from the Student Workbook. Tell them that this page will be used to see what they already know about the Words for the Week. Ask them to listen carefully to each word as you say it, repeat it in a sentence, and say it once again. Follow the procedures for this page as described in the *Introduction* at the beginning of this Teacher's Guide.

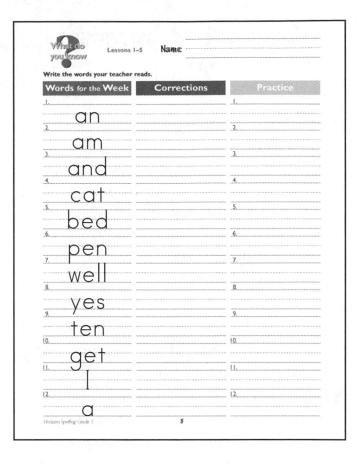

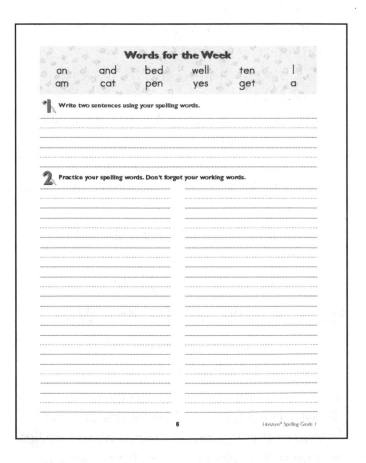

Lesson 1 - Introduce Words

Activities:

1. Give the students Lesson 1 and have the children look at the pictures. Ask them to give the name for each picture: **cat**, **bed**, **pen**, **ten**, **well**, **yes**. The last may be a little difficult. Point out that the girl is moving her head up and down as the arrows show.

2. Ask the children to write the spelling word for each picture on the line provided.

3. Ask the children to tell you which words on the list were not pictured.

4. Point out the words that are spelled with only one letter: **I**, **a**. Tell them that the word **I** is always capitalized. Tell them that the word **a** is a helping word called an "article." Give examples. Tell them that the word **an** is also an article and give examples.

5. Ask the children to add their Working Words to the word box and to write their Working Words for the week on their own paper.

6. Show the children how to write their Working Words in the appropriate section at the back of their *Spelling Dictionary*.

7. Remember that all pages should be removed from the Student Workbook to promote good penmanship.

Extended Activities for the Week:

1. Reproducible *Week 1 Worksheet* for in-class or take-home use.

2. Begin building recognition by working with word families. The words *am* and *and* in this lesson represent word families that will be developed in future lessons.

Other word families in this lesson and on the worksheet are -at, -an, -ed, -en, -ell, and -et.

Work with the children, or instruct parents to work with the children, to identify as many words as they can think of for each family.

3. Make a class word family chart for each family listed on the worksheet. Hang where children can see it. Add words as they are learned. Highlight or check off words that are part of spelling lessons or reading lessons.

4. Have the children begin a word family notebook. The word families can be written in either a spiral notebook or on loose-leaf paper that is placed into a 3-ring binder. There should be a separate page for each family.

Lesson 2 - Examine and Explore Words

Teaching Tips:

1. Review the rules for the week. (See the **Reproducible Phonics Rules Flashcards** at the end of this Teacher's Guide.)
2. Review the week's words in the box at the top of Lesson 2.

Activities:

1. Give the students Lesson 2. Read the directions for the first activity. Practice the short ă sound with the children.
2. Read the spelling words aloud. Ask the children to raise their hands when they hear words with the short ă sound.
3. Ask the children to point to the spelling words which will be written on the lines for this activity.

   Have the children write the words.
4. Read the direction for Activity 2. Ask the children to find the words and write them on the lines. Remind them that the word "I" is always spelled with a capital letter.
5. Read the direction for the third exercise. Practice the short ĕ sound.
6. Read the spelling words aloud. Ask the children to raise their hands when they hear words with the short ĕ sound.
7. Ask the children to find the words that have a short ĕ sound and write them on the lines.
8. Review the two words chosen for the Working Words. Write each word in a sentence. The sentences may be composed by the class or chosen by the teacher. Write the sentence on the board so that the children can copy them.

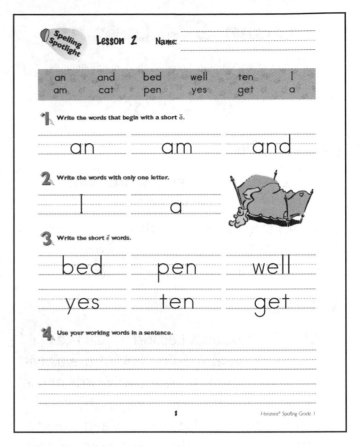

Extended Activities:

1. Continue work on word family charts or notebooks.
2. Continue work on Week 1 Worksheet.

Lesson 3 - Look at Context and Meaning of Words

Teaching Tips:

1. Review rules, Working Words, and spelling words as needed.

2. As an introduction to this page, help the children find their spelling words in their *Spelling Dictionary*.

Activities:

1. Give the students Lesson 3. Ask the children to look at the first line of the activity. Have them read the two words at the beginning of the line. Look at the sentence following the words. Read the sentence aloud, omitting the correct answer. Ask the children which of the two words at the beginning of the line finishes the sentence correctly. Read both options if needed. Instruct the children first to circle the correct word, then copy it in the space provided. Have the children read the completed sentence together.

2. Repeat this procedure for the remaining sentences. If any children are advanced enough, allow them to continue on their own. Check their work.

Bible Connection:

1. Discuss the picture with the children. What do they see? Who might the man be?

2. Read the story from Luke. Discuss the story with the children.

   a. What did Jesus do?

   b. How many men did he cure?

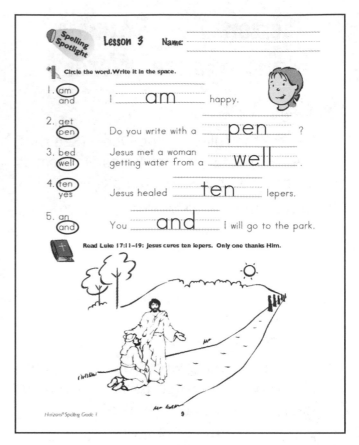

   c. What did they do after he cured them?

   d. How many were grateful for what he did?

   e. What did Jesus say to the man who returned?

3. Ask the children to point out any short ă or short ĕ words they heard in the story.

4. Have the children color the story and add any details they would like.

Extended Activity:

Review and continue work on word family charts or notebooks.

Lesson 4 - Apply Understanding of Words in Writing

Teaching Tips:

1. Review all words, rules, and Working Words for the week.
2. Review word family charts.

Activities:

1. Give the students Lesson 4. Ask them what they see in the picture. What is on the bed?

2. Read the directions above the box. Discuss what they might write about: color of bed, the cat on the bed, the color of the cat, the pen on the bed, and so on. Ask how the cat and the pen might have gotten on the bed.

3. Look at the box. If children are unfamiliar with a letter format, demonstrate on the board the parts of a letter. Write a sample letter on the board that does NOT relate to the assigned picture.

4. Ask the children to write their letter about the picture. Help as needed. Refer to word box and word family charts for help with spelling. Refer to *Spelling Dictionary* for other words.

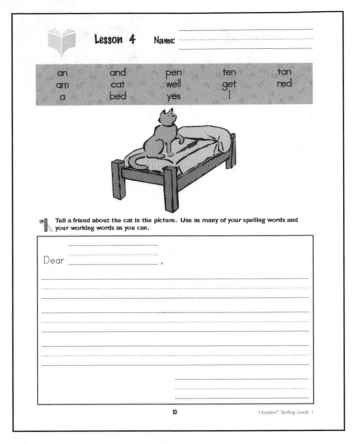

Extended Activities:

1. Make two sets of word cards for each spelling and Working Word.

2. Allow children to work in pairs. One child draws a word, then ask the other child to spell the word.

3. Word cards may also be placed face down and children can pick to find pairs of words.

Lesson 5 - Assess and Evaluate Progress

Activities:

1. Give the students Lesson 5. Tell the children that this is a "Check-up" page to see what they have learned during the week. [Note: Teachers/parents of home schoolers may decide what will be assessed. If a child did exceptionally well on the "What do you know?" pre-assessment, the teacher may choose not to test words already known by the child. Or the teacher may choose to test all Words for the Week.]

2. Tell the children that you will say a word. They will listen to the word and to the sentence you will give them. Then, they will write the word on the line next to the numbers. [Lines are given for the weekly words, but make sure to also check the Working Words for the week.]

3. Say the word. Repeat it in the context of a sentence. Repeat the word.

4. The children write the word dictated in the **Spelling Test** column.

5. The process is repeated until all words have been tested.

6. The teacher may correct in class by writing the words on the board and having the children compare or "self-correct" their work. Or the teacher may correct each child's work individually.

7. The teacher then uses the **Corrections** column to write any corrections for words misspelled.

8. In the **Practice** column, the child copies the correct spelling of any words missed.

9. The second side of the page can be used for retesting, for testing additional sight or "Working Words" added for the week, and for additional practice.

Extended Activity:

Review any words missed.

Week 2

Lessons 6-10: Assess Child's Knowledge

Goal: To recognize and spell short ĭ and short ŏ words. (See the **Reproducible Phonics Rules Flashcards** at the end of this Teacher's Guide.)

Short Vowel Rule: When a word or syllable has only one vowel, and it comes between two consonants, or at the beginning of the word or syllable, the vowel is usually short: **it**, **pin**, **bin**, **on**, **hot**.

What Do You Know?

Give the students the What do you know? page for Lessons 6-10. Tell them that this page will be used to see what they already know about the Words for the Week. Ask them to listen carefully to each word as you say it, repeat it in a sentence, and say it once again. Follow the procedures for this page as described in the *Introduction* at the beginning of this Teacher's Guide.

Ask the children to write their Working Words for the week in the word box and on their own paper.

Show the children how to write their Working Words in the appropriate section at the back of their *Spelling Dictionary*.

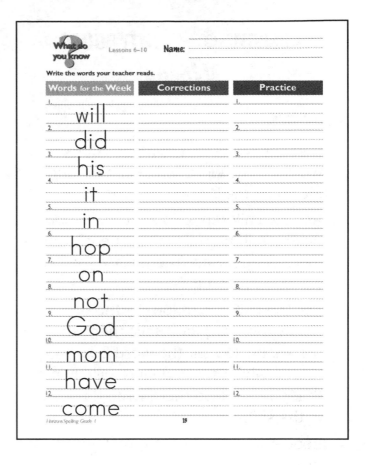

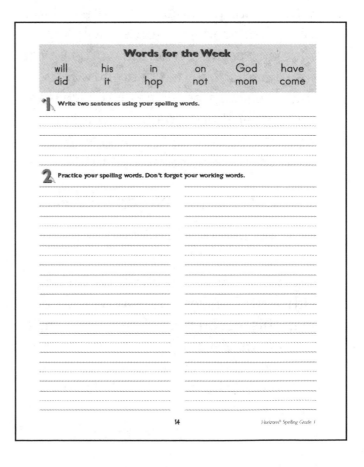

Lesson 6 - Introduce Words

Activities:

1. Give the students Lesson 6. Look at the words in the word box. Read all words, including the Working Words.

2. Ask the children to look at the shape boxes. Tell the children that each word has a shape. Have them trace the two words: **will** and **did**.

3. Ask the children to look at the box below the word **did**. Have them study the shape, look at the word box, and decide which spelling word will fit into that shape. Have them write the word in the shape boxes.

4. Repeat for each of the remaining shape boxes.

5. In the space provided, have the children write their Working Words, including **have** and **come**. Write the words on the board and show the children how to draw the shape boxes around each letter.

6. Remember that all pages should be removed from the Student Workbook to promote good penmanship

Extended Activities for the Week:

1. Reproducible *Week 2 Worksheet* for in-class or take-home use.

2. Begin building recognition by working with word families. The words *it*, *in,* and *on* in this lesson represent word families that will be developed in future lessons. Other word families in this lesson and on the worksheet are -ill, -id, -is, -op, -ot, -od, and -om.

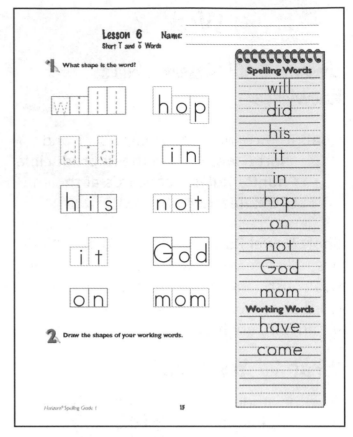

Work with the children, or instruct parents to work with the children, to identify as many words as they can think of for each family.

3. Make a class word family chart for each family listed on the worksheet. Hang where children can see it. Add words as they are learned. Highlight or check off words that are part of spelling lessons or reading lessons.

4. Have the children continue or begin a word family notebook. The word families can be written in either a spiral notebook or on loose-leaf paper that is placed into a 3-ring binder. There should be a separate page for each family.

Lesson 7 - Examine and Explore Words

Teaching Tip:

Review: Short vowel rule, Working Words, and words in word box.
(See the **Reproducible Phonics Rules Flashcards** at the end of this Teacher's Guide.)

Activities:

1. Give the students Lesson 7. Read the spelling words aloud. Ask the children to raise their hands when they hear words with the short ĭ sound.

2. Read the spelling words aloud. Ask the children to raise their hands when they hear words with the short ŏ sound.

3. Ask the students to take their pencils and draw a circle around all of the short ŏ words in the green box. Check. Make sure that any student who has circled **come** understands the difference between the **o** sound in **come** and the short ŏ sound.

4. Using the word family charts, practice words that rhyme. Then ask the children to listen to the first word, **lid**. What spelling word rhymes with **lid**? Have the children write the spelling word on the line.

5. Repeat for the remaining words in Activity 2.

6. Write the Working Words on the board. Ask the children to think of words that rhyme with them. Have the children write a rhyming word for each one on the line.

Extended Activity:

Continue work on word family sheets and charts. Children may want to begin a word family book at home. Taking one sheet for each family, write the family on the top of the sheet, add words or pictures which belong in the specific family. These sheets can be kept in a binder.

Lesson 8 - Look at Context and Meaning of Words

Teaching Tips:

1. Review words, Working Words and rule. (See the **Reproducible Phonics Rules Flashcards** at the end of this Teacher's Guide.)

2. Have the children find each spelling word in their *Spelling Dictionary*.

Activities:

1. Give the students Lesson 8. Ask the students to read the spelling words in the word box. Read the first sentence aloud, omitting the correct word. Ask the children which spelling word from the word box would complete the sentence. Have the children write the word in the sentence. Read the sentence together.

2. Repeat this process for the remaining sentences, allowing those children who are able to work independently.

3. Write the Bible verse on the board or make a banner for it. Read the verse aloud. Ask the children to read it with you. Talk about God's love and all the ways in which He shows His love. Have the children contribute ways in which they see God's love for them.

4. Ask the children to write the verse on the lines provided. Help them to judge the spacing they will need.

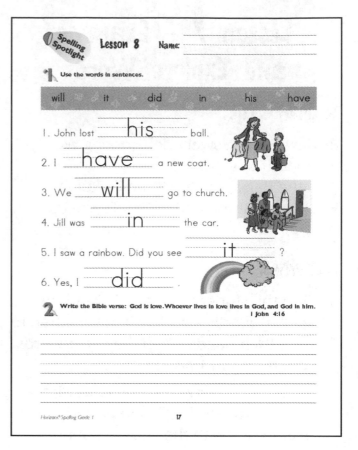

Extended Activity:

Have the children make a collage, either at school or at home, showing all the things God has provided in His love for us.

Lesson 9 - Apply Understanding of Words in Writing

Teaching Tip:

Review words, Working Words, and letter format.

Activities:

1. Give the students Lesson 9. Discuss the picture. Have the children talk about their mothers. Why are they thankful for their mothers?

2. Tell them that they will be writing another letter, this time to God. They will tell God about their mothers.

3. Have word family charts and *Spelling Dictionary* available. Help as needed.

4. When they have finished, they may read their letters.

Extended Activity:

Copy the letter on good paper, decorate it, and give it to Mom.

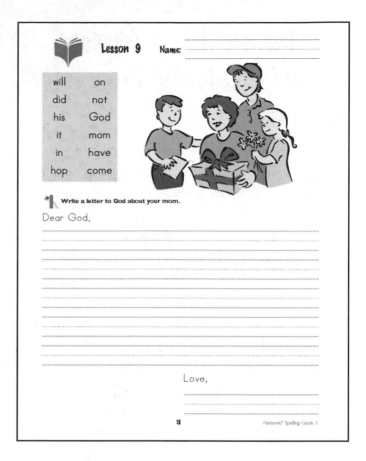

Lesson 10 - Assess and Evaluate Progress

Activities:

1. Give the students Lesson 10. Tell the children that this is a "Check-up" page to see what they have learned during the week. [Note: Teachers/parents of home schoolers may decide what will be assessed. If a child did exceptionally well on the "What do you know?" pre-assessment, the teacher may choose not to test words already known by the child. Or the teacher may choose to test all Words for the Week.]

2. Tell the children that you will say a word. They will listen to the word and to the sentence you will give them. Then, they will write the word on the line next to the numbers. [Lines are given for the weekly words, but make sure to also check the Working Words for the week.]

3. Say the word. Repeat it in the context of a sentence. Repeat the word.

4. The children write the word dictated in the **Test** column.

5. The process is repeated until all words have been tested.

6. The teacher may correct in class by writing the words on the board and having the children compare or "self-correct" their work. Or the teacher may correct each child's work individually.

7. The teacher then uses the **Correction** column to write any corrections for words misspelled.

8. In the **Practice** column, the child copies the correct spelling of any words missed.

9. The second side of the page can be used for retesting, for testing additional sight or "Working Words" added for the week, and for additional practice.

Extended Activity:

Review any words missed.

Week 3

Lessons 11-15: Assess Child's Knowledge

Goal: To recognize and spell short ŭ words and words with hard and soft **c** and **g**.

Review Short Vowel Rule: When a word or syllable has only one vowel, and it comes between two consonants or at the beginning of the word or syllable, the vowel is usually short: **up**, **run**, **but**.

Introduce Rule: When **c** is followed by **e**, **i**, or **y**, it makes the soft sound, as in the word "city." When **c** is followed by **a**, **u**, or **o** or a consonant, it makes the hard sound, as in the word "**cat**."

Introduce Rule: When **g** is followed by **e**, **i**, or **y**, it makes the soft sound, as in the word "**giraffe**." When **g** is followed by **a**, **u**, or **o** or a consonant, it makes the hard sound, as in the word "**gum**."

What Do You Know?

Give the students the What do you know? page for Lessons 11-15. Tell them that this page will be used to see what they already know about the Words for the Week. Ask them to listen carefully to each word as you say it, repeat it in a sentence, and say it once again. Follow the procedures for this page as described in the Introduction at the beginning of this Teacher's Guide.

Ask the children to write their Working Words for the week in the word box and on their own paper.

Show the children how to write their Working Words in the appropriate section at the back of their *Spelling Dictionary*.

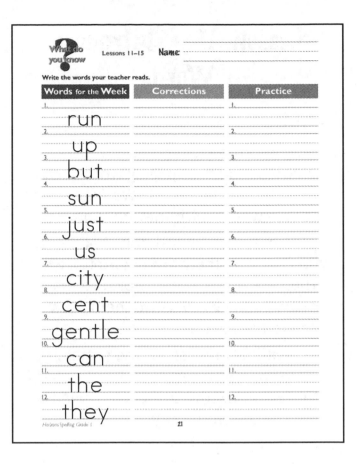

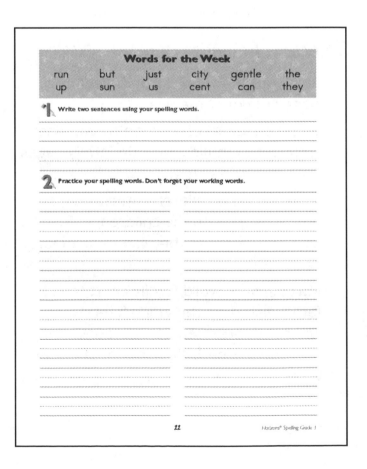

Lesson 11 - Introduce Words

Activities:

1. Give the students Lesson 11. Have the children read the spelling words in the word box, including the Working Words for the week which they have added.

2. Look at the first word, **run**. Ask the children to read the word and to trace it. Then ask them to find a picture that matches the word. Have them draw a line to the picture.

3. Repeat this process for the remaining words and pictures.
   NOTE: Review the soft **c** rule when you discuss the words **city** and **cent**.

4. Remember that all pages should be removed from the Student Workbook to promote good penmanship

Extended Activities for the Week:

1. Reproducible *Week 3 Worksheet* for in-class or take-home use.

   Begin building recognition by working with word families. Include family pages for soft **c** and soft **g**.

   Work with the children, or instruct parents to work with the children, to identify as many words as they can think of for each family.

2. Make a class word family chart for each family listed on the worksheet. Hang where children can see it. Add words as they are learned. Highlight or check off words that are part of spelling lessons or reading lessons.

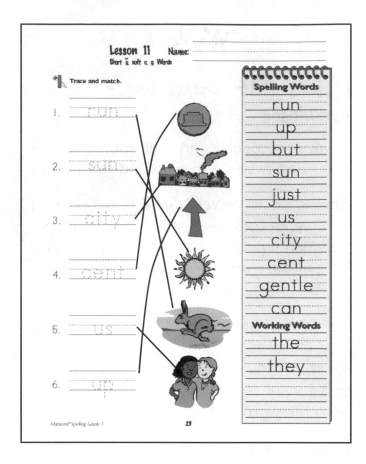

Lesson 12 - Examine and Explore Words

Teaching Tips:

1. Review rules, words, and Working Words.
2. Note the word **gentle** when reviewing the rule for soft **g**.

Activities:

1. Give the students Lesson 12. Have the children say all of the spelling words in the word box.
2. Ask them to listen carefully and find two spelling words that rhyme.
3. Ask them to write those two rhyming words on the lines in Activity 1.
4. Reading the words again, ask the children to find two soft **c** words. Write them on the lines in Activity 2.
5. Have the children find the two words beginning with **th** and write them on the lines in Activity 3.
6. Have the children find and write the one soft **g** word in Activity 4.
7. Have the children find and write the one hard **c** word in Activity 5.
8. Read all of the spelling words again. Ask the children to raise their hands when they hear a short **ŭ** sound. Have them take their pencils and circle the short **ŭ** words in the purple box.

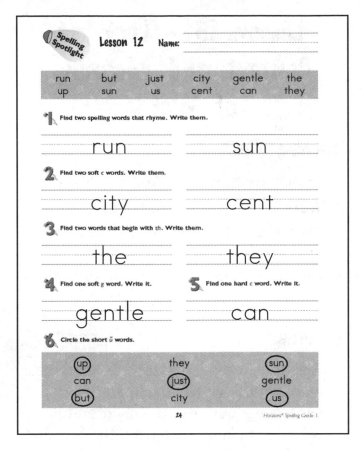

Extended Activity:

Continue work on word family sheets, charts, or notebooks.

Lesson 13 - Look at Context and Meaning of Words

Teaching Tips:

1. Review rules, words, Working Words.
2. Work with the children on opposite meanings: **high/low, long/short, big/little**, and so on.
3. Help the children to locate their spelling words in the *Spelling Dictionary*.

Activities:

1. Give the students Lesson 13. Read the words in the word box. Read the first sentence aloud. Ask the children to select a spelling word from the box that would replace the word walk in the sentence. Have them write the word on the line next to the sentence.
2. Repeat this process for the remaining sentences.
   NOTE: All words are opposites EXCEPT the words **penny/cent**, which are synonyms.
3. Read the Bible verse to the children. Ask them to recite it with you. Ask them to tell what other things God made.
4. On separate paper, ask the children to copy the Bible verse and decorate it with pictures of the sun, moon, and stars.

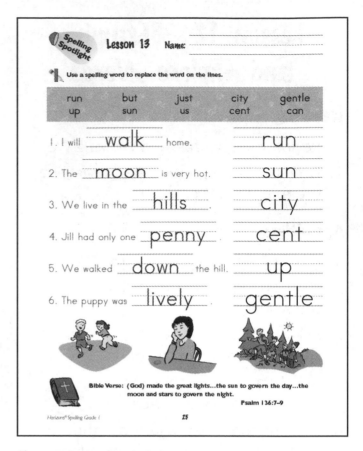

Extended Activity:

Have the children draw or draw/write about other things that God has made.

Lesson 14 - Apply Understanding of Words in Writing

Teaching Tips:

1. Review spelling words and Working Words.
2. Have word family charts and *Spelling Dictionary* at hand.

Activities:

1. Give the students Lesson 14. Ask the children to look at the picture of the city. What do they see that tells them this is a city? [If children live in the country, find some pictures of cities for them to study.]

2. Talk about possible stories for the picture. Who are the children? Do they have names? Are they friends or brother and sister? Where are they going? Is one of the houses their home? What kind of a day is it?

3. Ask the children to write their own stories about the city, using as many spelling words as they can. Help as needed. Praise all efforts.

Extended Activity:

Have children find city pictures in magazines or papers and make a poster.

Lesson 15 - Assess and Evaluate Progress

Activities:

1. Give the students Lesson 15. Tell the children that this is a "Check-up" page to see what they have learned during the week. [Note: Teachers/parents of home schoolers may decide what will be assessed. If a child did exceptionally well on the "What do you know?" pre-assessment, the teacher may choose not to test words already known by the child. Or the teacher may choose to test all Words for the Week.]

2. Tell the children that you will say a word. They will listen to the word and to the sentence you will give them. Then, they will write the word on the line next to the numbers. [Lines are given for the weekly words, but make sure to also check the Working Words for the week.]

3. Say the word. Repeat it in the context of a sentence. Repeat the word.

4. The children write the word dictated in the **Test** column.

5. The process is repeated until all words have been tested.

6. The teacher may correct in class by writing the words on the board and having the children compare or "self-correct" their work. Or the teacher may correct each child's work individually.

7. The teacher then uses the **Correction** column to write any corrections for words misspelled.

8. In the **Practice** column, the child copies the correct spelling of any words missed.

9. The second side of the page can be used for retesting, for testing additional sight or "Working Words" added for the week, and for additional practice.

Extended Activity:

Review any words missed.

Week 4

Lessons 16-20: Assess Child's Knowledge

Goal: To recognize and spell words with the long $\bar{a}$ sound.

Introduce: Long vowel rule: When a word or syllable has two vowels, the first vowel is usually long and the second vowel is usually silent: **name**, **pain**, **pay**. (See the **Reproducible Phonics Rules Flashcards** at the end of this Teacher's Guide.)

Introduce: Long vowel mark ($^-$).

What Do You Know?

Give the students the What do you know? page for Lessons 16-20. Tell them that this page will be used to see what they already know about the Words for the Week. Ask them to listen carefully to each word as you say it, repeat it in a sentence, and say it once again. Follow the procedures for this page as described in the *Introduction* at the beginning of this Teacher's Guide.

Ask the children to write their Working Words for the week in the word box and on their own paper.

Show the children how to write their Working Words in the appropriate section at the back of their *Spelling Dictionary*.

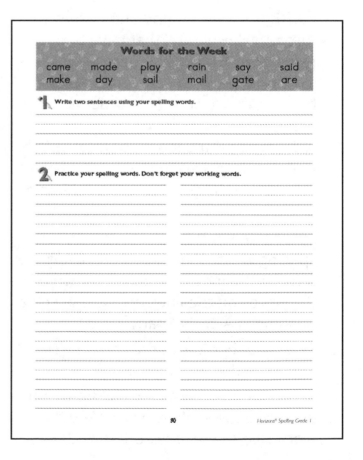

Lesson 16 - Introduce Words

Activities:

1. Give the students Lesson 16. Explain to the children that the sound for long ā can be spelled in different ways. Tell them that in this lesson, they will learn three ways to spell the long ā sound. Look at the word list. Read the words with the children. Ask for their observations on the differences in spelling the words. See how many observe that some words have an __a__ e patterns; others have an __ay pattern; and still others have an __ai__ pattern.

2. Ask the children to find four spelling words which have the __a_e pattern. Ask them to write those words in the four spaces provided under the red line in Activity 1 (any order is acceptable).

3. Ask the children to find and to read the three spelling words that have the __ai__ pattern for long ā. Ask them to write the words on the lines beneath the orange heading in Activity 1 (any order is acceptable).
   NOTE: Here is a good place to point out that the word **said** may look like the others, but is NOT pronounced as a long ā word.

4. Ask the children to find the three spelling words that have the __ay pattern for the long ā. Ask them to write the words on the lines beneath the blue heading in Activity 1 (any order).

5. Read Number 2 with the children. Find and write the spelling word.

6. Read Number 3 with the children. Find and write the spelling word. (Add the word **said** to the short ě family chart.)

Extended Activities for the Week:

1. Reproducible *Week 4 Worksheet* for in-class or take-home use.

   Begin building recognition by working with word families. Make a long ā family page which is divided into different ways to spell the long ā sound.

   Work with the children, or instruct parents to work with the children, to identify as many words as they can think of for each family. Add the word **said** to the short ě page. Begin a page for **ar** words.

2. Make a class word family chart for each family listed on the worksheet. Hang where children can see it. Add words as they are learned. Highlight or check off words that are part of spelling lessons or reading lessons.

3. Write sentences with the Working Words chosen for the week.

Lesson 17 - Examine and Explore Words

Teaching Tip:

Review spelling words, Working Words, and rules. (See the **Reproducible Phonics Rules Flashcards** at the end of this Teacher's Guide.)

Activities:

1. Give the students Lesson 17. Look at the first six pictures. Name them. Ask the children to find the spelling word that describes the first picture (**gate**). Ask the children to write the word under the picture. Continue this process for the remaining pictures. If a child is able to complete independently, allow him/her to do so.

2. In Activity 2, the children are looking for spelling words that will rhyme with the pictures given. Have them say the name of the picture (**bed, cake, game**). Have them find the spelling word that rhymes with the picture (**said, make, came**). Have them write the spelling word under the picture.

Extended Activities:

1. Continue work on word family sheets, charts, or notebooks for the week.

2. Use Working Words and spelling words in original sentences.

Lesson 18 - Look at Context and Meaning of Words

Teaching Tips:

1. Help the children to locate their spelling words in the *Spelling Dictionary*.

2. Review spelling words, Working Words, and rules for the week. (See the **Reproducible Phonics Rules Flashcards** at the end of this Teacher's Guide.)

Activities:

1. Give the students Lesson 18. Review the concept of opposites with the children. Use spelling words from this and other units as examples.

2. Tell the children that they will be looking for **opposites** in the first activity.
NOTE: Have them refer to the word list from Lesson 17 in completing this activity. Look at the pictures. Read the words given. Ask the children what spelling word explains the opposite of the word **night**? Have them write the word **day** on the line next to the word **night**. Repeat the process for the remaining three pictures and words.

3. Read the directions for Activity 2 with the children. Ask the children to read the words in the word box. Read the first sentence aloud, omitting the correct answer words. Ask the children which two words from the word box will complete the sentence correctly. Have the children write the correct words on the lines provided in the first sentence. Repeat the process for the remaining sentences.

4. Discuss the punctuation used in the sentences. Note the quotation marks, comma, question marks, and the period.

5. Point out the use of capital letters for names, beginning of sentences, and the beginning of a quotation.

6. Read the Bible verse to the children. Ask them to repeat it with you. Go to John, Chapter 10 for the entire quotation and read it to the children. Provide paper for the children that will allow room to write the quote and to illustrate it.

Extended Activity:

Write a variety of sentences: questions, quotation, exclamations, with the children using spelling words and Working Words from all units to date. Highlight the use of capital letters and specific punctuation. (See the **Reproducible Phonics Rules Flashcards** at the end of this Teacher's Guide.)

Lesson 19 - Apply Understanding of Words in Writing

Teaching Tip:

Review spelling words, Working Words, and rules. (See the **Reproducible Phonics Rules Flashcards** at the end of this Teacher's Guide.)

Activities:

1. Give the students Lesson 19. Ask the children what they see in the picture. Ask them about specific details in the picture (the open gate, the puddle, the rain, the mail being delivered, and so on).

2. Encourage the children to write a story about the picture that will describe some of the details just discussed. Ask them to use the spelling words in the box, Working Words, and their own words to complete the story. Help as needed.

3. Encourage children to use their *Spelling Dictionary* to find words that they do not know or words they have studied but have forgotten.

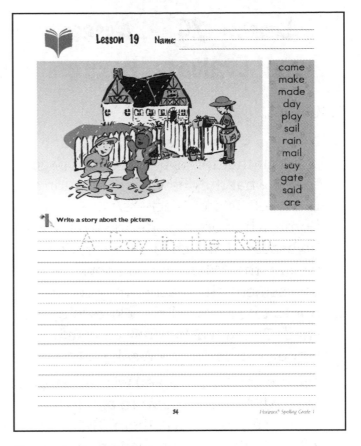

Extended Activity:

Review spelling words, Working Words, and word family pages.

Lesson 20 - Assess and Evaluate Progress

Activities:

1. Give the students Lesson 20. Tell the children that this is a "Check-up" page to see what they have learned during the week. [Note: Teachers/parents of home schoolers may decide what will be assessed. If a child did exceptionally well on the "What do you know?" pre-assessment, the teacher may choose not to test words already known by the child. Or the teacher may choose to test all Words for the Week.]

2. Tell the children that you will say a word. They will listen to the word and to the sentence you will give them. Then, they will write the word on the line next to the numbers. [Lines are given for the weekly words, but make sure to also check the Working Words for the week.]

3. Say the word. Repeat it in the context of a sentence. Repeat the word.

4. The children write the word dictated in the **Test** column.

5. The process is repeated until all words have been tested.

6. The teacher may correct in class by writing the words on the board and having the children compare or "self-correct" their work. Or the teacher may correct each child's work individually.

7. The teacher then uses the **Correction** column to write any corrections for words misspelled.

8. In the **Practice** column, the child copies the correct spelling of any words missed.

9. The second side of the page can be used for retesting, for testing additional sight or "Working Words" added for the week, and for additional practice.

Extended Activity:

Review any words missed.

Week 5

Lessons 21-25: Assess Child's Knowledge

Goal: To recognize and spell words with the long ē sound. (See the **Reproducible Phonics Rules Flashcards** at the end of this Teacher's Guide.)

Introduce Rule: When a word or syllable has just one vowel, and the vowel comes at the end of the word or syllable, the vowel sound is usually long: **be, go, Tony.**

Review and apply to long ē: Rule: When a word or syllable has two vowels, the first vowel is usually long and the second vowel is usually silent: **meet, weak.**

What Do You Know?

Give the students the What do you know? page for Lessons 21-25. Tell them that this page will be used to see what they already know about the Words for the Week. Ask them to listen carefully to each word as you say it, repeat it in a sentence, and say it once again. Follow the procedures for this page as described in the *Introduction* at the beginning of this Teacher's Guide.

Ask the children to write their Working Words for the week in the word box and on their own paper.

Show the children how to write their Working Words in the appropriate section at the back of their *Spelling Dictionary*.

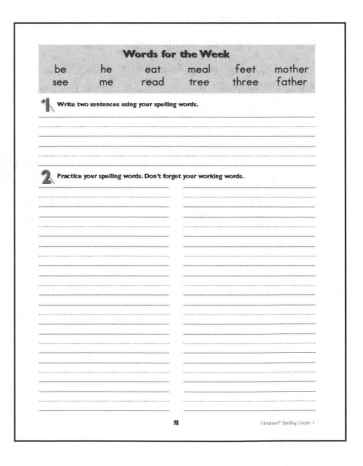

Lesson 21 - Introduce Words

Activities:

1. Give the students Lesson 21. Explain to the children that the sound for long $\bar{e}$ can be spelled in different ways. Tell them that in this lesson, they will learn three ways to spell the long $\bar{e}$ sound. Look at the word list. Read the words with the children. Ask for their observations on the differences in spelling the words. See how many observe that some words have an __ee pattern; others have an __ea pattern; and still others have an __e pattern.

2. Ask the children to find and read the four spelling words that have the **ee** spelling for the long $\bar{e}$ sound. Ask them to write these words on the lines below the direction in Activity 1 (any order).

3. Ask the children to find the three words that spell the long $\bar{e}$ sound using the **ea** pattern. Which word also goes with the picture? Ask the children to write the three words on the lines provided in Activity 2 (any order).

4. Ask the children to find the three words that use the __e pattern to spell the long $\bar{e}$ sound. Have them select two of those words to write on the lines provided in Activity 3 (any order).

5. Look at the picture in Activity 4. What does it show? Read the direction with the children. Have them read and write the spelling words for this activity on the lines provided.

6. Ask the children to write the remaining Working Words for the week on the lines provided in Activity 5.

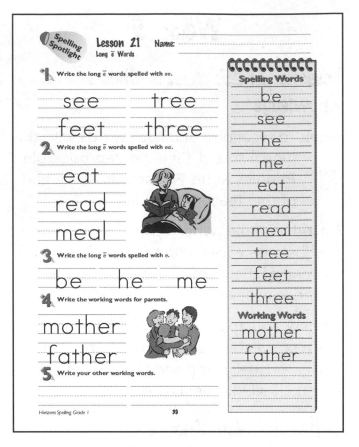

Extended Activities for the Week:

1. Reproducible *Week 5 Worksheet* for in-class or take-home use. Begin building recognition by working with word families. Make a long $\bar{e}$ family page which is divided into different ways to spell the long $\bar{e}$ sound. Work with the children, or instruct parents to work with the children, to identify as many words as they can think of for each family. Begin a sheet for words that tell of family relationships: mother, father, sister, brother, aunt, uncle, grandfather, grandmother, etc.

2. Make a class word family chart for each family listed on the worksheet. Hang where children can see it. Add words as they are learned. Highlight or check off words that are part of spelling lessons or reading lessons.

3. Write sentences with the Working Words chosen for the week. Add Working Words to family charts already made, or begin new ones to fit the patterns of the Working Words.

Lesson 22 - Examine and Explore Words

Teaching Tip:

Review spelling words, Working Words, and rules for the week. (See the **Reproducible Phonics Rules Flashcards** at the end of this Teacher's Guide.)

Activities:

1. Give the students Lesson 22. Have the children read the words in the word box. Look at the pictures. Review the pictures. Ask the children to find the spelling word that describes the first picture (**he**). Have them write the word below the picture. Continue this process for the remaining pictures. If a child is able to work independently, allow it.

2. Read the Bible verse. Ask the children to read it with you. Talk about ways in which they honor their parents. Have them copy the verse and illustrate at least one way in which they show honor to their parents.

Extended Activities:

1. Have the children add the words from the Bible verse to the appropriate word family pages.

2. Continue work on word families for this week.

Lesson 23 - Look at Context and Meaning of Words

Teaching Tips:

1. Help the children to locate their spelling words in the *Spelling Dictionary*.
2. Review spelling words, Working Words, and rules for the week.

Activities:

1. Give the students Lesson 23. Ask the children to read all of the spelling words in the word box.

2. What do these words have in common? (They rhyme.)

3. Tell the children that they will use these rhyming words to complete the four sentences in the first activity. Read the first sentence and ask the children which word from the box would best complete the sentence. Have the children write the word (**he**) in the space provided. Repeat the process for the remaining sentences. Note question marks, apostrophes, and the capitalization of names and the first word in a sentence.

4. Read the direction for Activity 2. Tell the children that they will have to decide which of the two words given in front of each sentence best completes the sentence. Read the two words in front of the first sentence. Read the sentence. Ask the children which word completes the sentence correctly. Have the children circle the correct word and then copy it on the line provided. Continue this process for the remaining sentences.

Extended Activity:

If children had difficulty with Activity 2 on this page, do more of the same on the board or as individual practice.

Lesson 24 - Apply Understanding of Words in Writing

Teaching Tips:

1. Review spelling words, Working Words, and rules.

2. Review word family pages and charts for this week.

Activities:

1. Give the students Lesson 24. Look at the picture. What is the family doing? What might be in the bowl mother is opening? What is in the bowl father is carrying? What is the boy eating? What is the baby doing?

2. Using the spelling words in the blue box, the Working Words for the week, any spelling words learned in previous lessons, and the *Spelling Dictionary*, ask the children to write a short story about the picture. Help as needed.

3. Share the stories with the class.

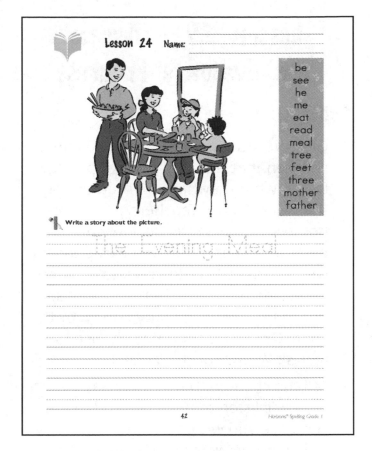

Lesson 25 - Assess and Evaluate Progress

Activities:

1. Give the students Lesson 25. Tell the children that this is a "Check-up" page to see what they have learned during the week. [Note: Teachers/parents of home schoolers may decide what will be assessed. If a child did exceptionally well on the "What do you know?" pre-assessment, the teacher may choose not to test words already known by the child. Or the teacher may choose to test all Words for the Week.]

2. Tell the children that you will say a word. They will listen to the word and to the sentence you will give them. Then, they will write the word on the line next to the numbers. [Lines are given for the weekly words, but make sure to also check the Working Words for the week.]

3. Say the word. Repeat it in the context of a sentence. Repeat the word.

4. The children write the word dictated in the **Test** column.

5. The process is repeated until all words have been tested.

6. The teacher may correct in class by writing the words on the board and having the children compare or "self-correct" their work. Or the teacher may correct each child's work individually.

7. The teacher then uses the **Correction** column to write any corrections for words misspelled.

8. In the **Practice** column, the child copies the correct spelling of any words missed.

9. The second side of the page can be used for retesting, for testing additional sight or "Working Words" added for the week, and for additional practice.

Extended Activity:

Review any words missed.

Week 6

Lessons 26-30: Assess Child's Knowledge

Goal: To recognize and spell words with the long ī sound.

Review: Rule: When a word or syllable has two vowels, the first vowel is usually long and the second vowel is usually silent: **kite**, **mile**.

Introduce: Rule: Sometimes **y** can make the long ē or **i** sound. The **y** is usually at the end of the word when it makes the long ē or **i** sound. (See the **Reproducible Phonics Rules Flashcards** at the end of this Teacher's Guide.)

What Do You Know?

Give the students the What do you know? page for Lessons 26-30. Tell them that this page will be used to see what they already know about the Words for the Week. Ask them to listen carefully to each word as you say it, repeat it in a sentence, and say it once again. Follow the procedures for this page as described in the *Introduction* at the beginning of this Teacher's Guide.

Ask the children to write their Working Words for the week in the word box and on their own paper.

Show the children how to write their Working Words in the appropriate section at the back of their *Spelling Dictionary*.

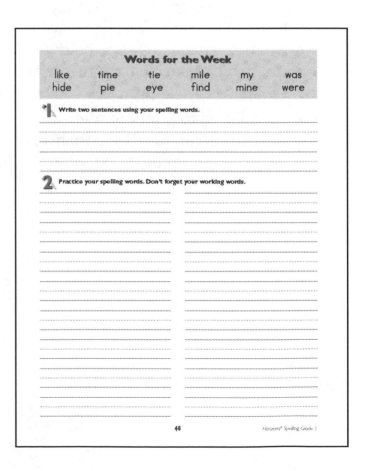

Lesson 26 - Introduce Words

Activities:

1. Give the students Lesson 26. Review word shapes with the children by putting some spelling words from a previous lesson on the board and drawing the shapes around them.

2. Look at the word shapes in Activity 1. Have the children note that the shapes in each line are the same. Tell them to look carefully at the spelling words in the box and to find two words with the same shape as they see in Activity 1. Write the words in the box. Have them look for two more words with the same shape as Number 2 in the first activity. Write the words.

3. In Activity 2, have the children study the words and the shapes, write each word in the correct shape. Instruct the children to then draw a line from the word to its shape.

4. Ask the children to print out their Working Words carefully. Help them to draw the shapes around these words.

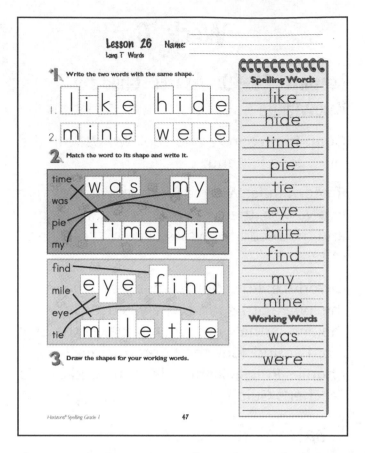

Extended Activities for the Week:

1. Reproducible *Week 6 Worksheet* for in-class or take-home use.

   Begin building recognition by working with word families. Make a long ī family page which is divided into different ways to spell the long ī sound.

   Work with the children, or instruct parents to work with the children, to identify as many words as they can think of for each family.

2. Make a class word family chart for each family listed on the worksheet. Hang where children can see it. Add words as they are learned. Highlight or check off words that are part of spelling lessons or reading lessons.

3. Write sentences with the Working Words chosen for the week.

Lesson 27 - Examine and Explore Words

Teaching Tip:

Review rules, spelling words, and Working Words.

Activities:

1. Give the students Lesson 27. Read the words in the word box. Tell the children that the first activity has words from the box hidden in a line of letters.

2. Look at the first one. Help the children to see the hidden word (**tie**) if they have a problem. Ask them to circle the spelling word. Have them write it on the line provided. Repeat this process for the remaining four words.

3. Demonstrate for the children how they can change a word from a short vowel sound to a new word with a long vowel sound by adding a silent **e**. Examples: **mat/mate, pan/pane, bar/bare, bid/bide**, and so on. Write the word **hid** on the board. Ask the children what happens if you add a silent **e** to the end of this word: **hid/hide**. What new word is formed? Is this new word a spelling word? Ask them to write the word in the space provided. Repeat the process with the word **Tim**.

4. The third activity asks the children to write the two words beginning with a **w**. Use this opportunity to demonstrate to the children how these little words are used in sentences and how important they are.

5. Have the children read all the words in the word box another time. Ask them to notice which words rhyme. Note that

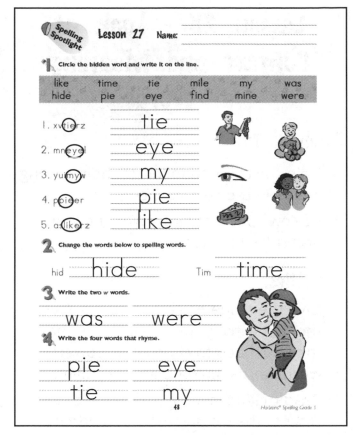

words can rhyme without looking the same or having exactly the same spelling. Ask the children to write the words in the spaces provided.

6. Note for the children the different spellings of the long ī sound: __i__e, __ie, and the letter **y** used as a long ī.

Extended Activities:

1. Continue work on word families for the week.

2. If children have difficulty with rhyming words, give additional practice.

3. Taking the short vowel family charts, see how many words can be changed to new words by adding a second silent vowel. Adjust or add to charts accordingly.

Lesson 28 - Look at Context and Meaning of Words

Teaching Tips:

1. Help the children to locate their spelling words in the *Spelling Dictionary*.
2. Review spelling words, Working Words, and rules for the week.

Activities:

1. Give the studetns Lesson 28. Look at the first activity. Tell the children that they will need to choose the correct word/words to complete each sentence.

2. Read the first sentence with the children. Discuss the picture. Ask the children to point to the word that will complete the sentence. Check. Have the children circle the correct word and then copy it in the space provided. Repeat this process for the remaining four sentences. Note questions, commas, capitalization of names, and the first word in a sentence.

3. Brainstorm some sentences for this week's Working Words. Write them on the board. The children may choose to copy one of these sentences or to write one of their own.

4. Read the Bible verse to the children. Have them recite it with you. Discuss its meaning with the children and God's care for us and goodness towards us. Have the children write the verse on separate paper and write about a way in which God has helped or protected them.

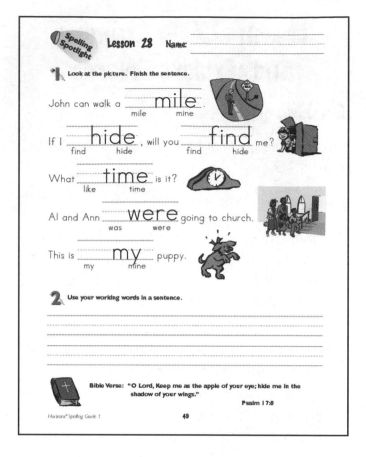

Extended Activity:

Add any words from the verse that are not yet included on word family pages.

Lesson 29 - Apply Understanding of Words in Writing

Teaching Tip:

Review all spelling words, Working Words, and rules for this lesson.

Activities:

1. Give the students Lesson 29. Ask the children if they have ever played the game of Hide and Seek. Have them describe the game and what they did. Where did they hide? Were they found quickly?

2. Discuss the picture in detail. Who is hiding? How many are already hidden? Where are they hiding? Who will be seeking? What is his name?

3. Using spelling words, Working Words, their *Spelling Dictionary*, and words from earlier lessons, ask the children to write about the game of Hide and Seek in the picture. Help as needed.

4. Share stories with the class.

Lesson 30 - Assess and Evaluate Progress

Activities:

1. Give the students Lesson 30. Tell the children that this is a "Check-up" page to see what they have learned during the week. [Note: Teachers/parents of home schoolers may decide what will be assessed. If a child did exceptionally well on the "What do you know?" pre-assessment, the teacher may choose not to test words already known by the child. Or the teacher may choose to test all Words for the Week.]

2. Tell the children that you will say a word. They will listen to the word and to the sentence you will give them. Then, they will write the word on the line next to the numbers. [Lines are given for the weekly words, but make sure to also check the Working Words for the week.]

3. Say the word. Repeat it in the context of a sentence. Repeat the word.

4. The children write the word dictated in the **Test** column.

5. The process is repeated until all words have been tested.

6. The teacher may correct in class by writing the words on the board and having the children compare or "self-correct" their work. Or the teacher may correct each child's work individually.

7. The teacher then uses the **Correction** column to write any corrections for words misspelled.

8. In the **Practice** column, the child copies the correct spelling of any words missed.

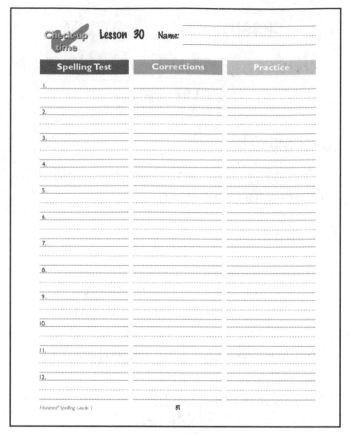

9. The second side of the page can be used for retesting, for testing additional sight or "Working Words" added for the week, and for additional practice.

Extended Activity:

Review any words missed.

Week 7

Lessons 31-35: Assess Child's Knowledge

Goal: To recognize and spell words with the long ō sound.

Review Rule: When a word or syllable has just one vowel, and the vowel comes at the end of the word or syllable, the vowel sound is usually long—**go, Tony.**

Review Rule: When a word or syllable has two vowels, the first vowel is usually long and the second vowel is usually silent—**home.**

What Do You Know?

Give the students the What do you know? page for Lessons 31-35. Tell them that this page will be used to see what they already know about the Words for the Week. Ask them to listen carefully to each word as you say it, repeat it in a sentence, and say it once again. Follow the procedures for this page as described in the *Introduction* at the beginning of this Teacher's Guide.

Ask the children to write their Working Words for the week in the word box and on their own paper.

Show the children how to write their Working Words in the appropriate section at the back of their *Spelling Dictionary*.

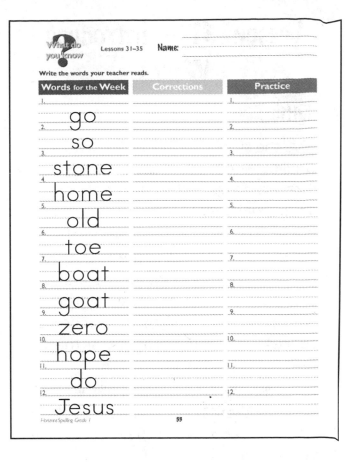

Lesson 31 - Introduce Words

Activities:

1. Give the students Lesson 31. Read the spelling words with the children. Note the three spellings of the long ō sound: __o, o__e, __oa__. Write the words on the board according to the different spellings.

2. Look at the pictures in the first activity. Find the spelling word for the first picture. What vowels are missing from the word? Write the vowels in the correct spaces. Repeat the process for the remaining pictures.

3. Have the children write all of the Working Words on the lines provided. Check to see that they have circled the vowels correctly.

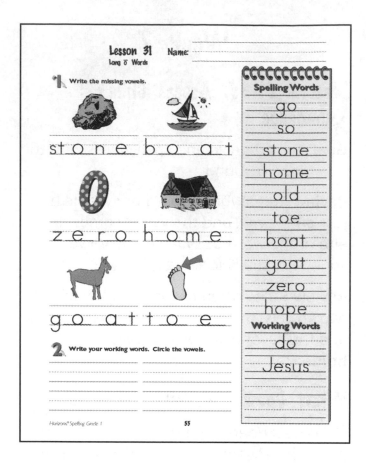

Extended Activities for the Week:

1. Reproducible *Week 7 Worksheet* for in-class or take-home use.

   Begin building recognition by working with word families. Make a long ō family page which is divided into different ways to spell the long ō sound.

   Work with the children, or instruct parents to work with the children, to identify as many words as they can think of for each family. Add the word Jesus to both the long ē and short ŭ pages if it is not already there.

2. Make a class word family chart for each family listed on the worksheet. Hang where children can see it. Add words as they are learned. Highlight or check off words that are part of spelling lessons or reading lessons.

3. Write sentences with the Working Words chosen for the week.

Lesson 32 - Examine and Explore Words

Teaching Tip:

Review spelling words, Working Words, and rules for the week.

Activities:

1. Give the students Lesson 32. Look at the picture. Look at the purple word box and have the children read the spelling words. Color the pictures. Draw a line from the word in the box to the picture that goes with the word.

2. In Activity 2, the children will sort the spelling words according to the long $\bar{o}$ spelling of each word.

NOTE: Activity 2 is not related to the illustration in Activity 1. To complete this activity, the students should use the Words for the Week from the previous lesson or the word box on Lesson 33 for a complete list of spelling words.

Extended Activities:

1. Add to word family sheets.

2. Ask the children to create a story to go with the picture on the page.

Lesson 33 - Look at Context and Meaning of Words

Teaching Tips:

1. Help the children to locate their spelling words in the *Spelling Dictionary*.

2. Review spelling words, Working Words, and rules for the week.

Activities:

1. Give the students Lesson 33. Have the children read the spelling words in the box.

2. Tell them that they will use words from the box to complete the sentences in this activity. They will not use all of the words, but only those which complete the sentences correctly.

3. Read the first sentence, omitting the final word. Ask the children which spelling word best completes the sentence. Have the children write the word in the space provided. Repeat this process for the remaining sentences.

Extended Activity:

Have the children go to their *Spelling Dictionary*. Ask them to find the words that they have used in the sentences on this page. What does the dictionary tell them about these words? Read the sentences given in the dictionary for each word.

Lesson 34 - Apply Understanding of Words in Writing

Teaching Tip:

Review rules, spelling words, and Working Words.

Activities:

1. Give the student Lesson 34. Have a list of spelling words and Working Words available for the children.

2. Read the story from Luke. Talk about it with the children. What kind of a boat were they in? What would it feel like to be in such a bad storm? What did Jesus do? How can Jesus help us when we are in a "storm" or have trouble in our lives?

3. Ask the children to draw their favorite part of the story.

4. Ask them to write a letter to a friend telling them about the miracle Jesus worked.
   NOTE: Have the children help you make a list of words on the board that may be needed for their letters. Review letter format.

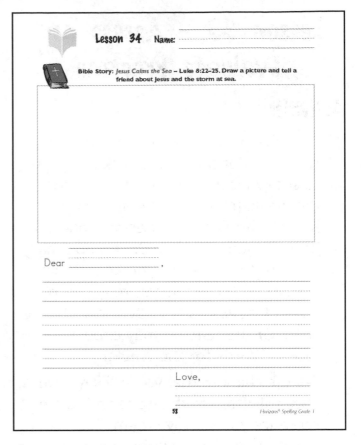

Lesson 34 Name:

Bible Story: *Jesus Calms the Sea – Luke 8:22–25.* Draw a picture and tell a friend about Jesus and the storm at sea.

Dear _____,

Love,

58   *Horizons® Spelling Grade 1*

Extended Activity:

Have the children create their own booklet in which they illustrate and write about the Bible story.

Lesson 35 - Assess and Evaluate Progress

Activities:

1. Give the student Lesson 35. Tell the children that this is a "Check-up" page to see what they have learned during the week. [Note: Teachers/parents of home schoolers may decide what will be assessed. If a child did exceptionally well on the "What do you know?" pre-assessment, the teacher may choose not to test words already known by the child. Or the teacher may choose to test all Words for the Week.]

2. Tell the children that you will say a word. They will listen to the word and to the sentence you will give them. Then, they will write the word on the line next to the numbers. [Lines are given for the weekly words, but make sure to also check the Working Words for the week.]

3. Say the word. Repeat it in the context of a sentence. Repeat the word.

4. The children write the word dictated in the **Test** column.

5. The process is repeated until all words have been tested.

6. The teacher may correct in class by writing the words on the board and having the children compare or "self-correct" their work. Or the teacher may correct each child's work individually.

7. The teacher then uses the **Correction** column to write any corrections for words misspelled.

8. In the **Practice** column, the child copies the correct spelling of any words missed.

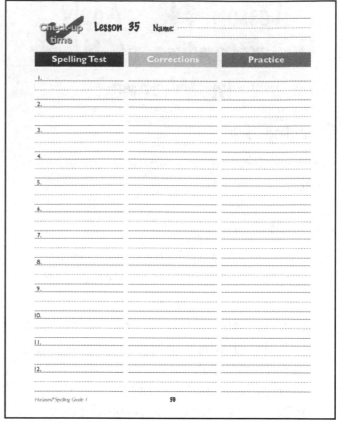

9. The second side of the page can be used for retesting, for testing additional sight or "Working Words" added for the week, and for additional practice.

Extended Activity:

Review any words missed.

Week 8

Lessons 36-40: Assess Child's Knowledge

Goal: Review words and patterns from Lessons 1–35.

(Include all rules taught to this point in this section.)

What Do You Remember?

Give the student the What do you remember? page for Lessons 1–35. Tell them that this page will be used to see what they remember about the words they have studied so far this year. Select an additional 4–6 Working Words from the list of words added each week. Ask them to listen carefully to each word as you say it, repeat it in a sentence, and say it once again. Follow the procedures for this page as described in the *Introduction* at the beginning of this Teacher's Guide.

NOTE: If you have kept records of words that each child continues to find difficult, you may want to adjust the words in this unit to fit the needs of the individual child. Replace review words already mastered with those still needing work.

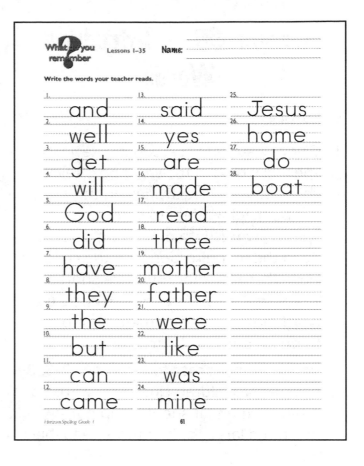

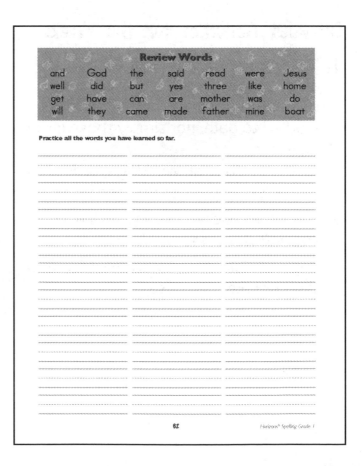

Lesson 36 - Introduce Words

Activities:

1. Give the students Lesson 36. Review the spelling words in the word box. Tell the children that the activities on this page will be helping them to sort out the spelling words into different groups. Read the first direction with the children. Have them look for the three short **ă** words in the list. Ask them to circle the words when they find them and to write them on the lines in Activity 1.

2. Repeat this process for Activities 2–8. By having the children circle the words as they use them, it should help narrow down the large list into more readable parts.

Extended Activities for the Week:

1. Use the sheets, charts, or booklets created for the word family exercises to help the children review all the words studied to date, not simply those included in the lesson. Include all Working Words given in the weeks prior to this one.

2. Have the children use the review spelling words in sentences.

3. Reproducible *Week 8 Worksheet* for in-class or take-home use.

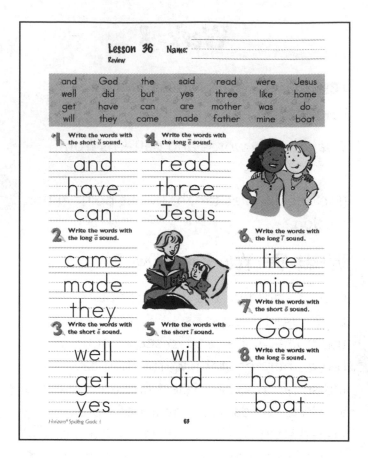

Lesson 37 - Examine and Explore Words

Activities:

1. Give the students Lesson 37. If children have difficulty with the large number of words in the box, select the words needed for the first activity and an additional 3 or 4 words for the children to give the children a shorter list from which to choose.

2. Read the sentences with the children. Tell them that it is a conversation between Jill and her mother. Note the questions marks, commas, quotation marks, and use of capitals. (See the **Reproducible Phonics Rules Flashcards** at the end of this Teacher's Guide regarding punctuation rules.) Ask the children to choose the spelling words needed to complete the conversation. Have the children write the words in the appropriate spaces.

3. Review rhyming words as needed. Ask the children to read each word in Activity 2 carefully and to select a spelling word that rhymes with the word printed in the list. Ask the children to write the rhyming word next to the printed word on the line provided. Do together or independently as children are able.

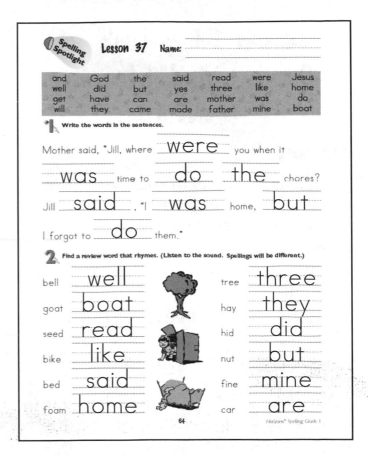

Lesson 38 - Look at Context and Meaning of Words

Teaching Tips:

1. Review the use of the dictionary. Talk about the arrangement of words in alphabetical (**ABC**) order. Have the children look at all of the Working Words they have entered into the back portion of their dictionary.

2. Review what children already know about sentences: capital letters, periods/question marks, and so on.

Activities:

1. Give the students Lesson 38. Tell the children that on this page they will practice writing sentences using some of their review spelling words.

2. Have the children read the two words for the first sentence: **Jesus**, **father**. Ask them to think of a sentence in which they could use both spelling words. Write examples on the board if needed. Have the children write their sentence on the line provided. Repeat the process for the remaining three sentences.

3. Explain to the children that they have been using their *Spelling Dictionary* now for seven weeks. This next activity is to help them become better at using their dictionaries. Write the words **like**, **are**, **was**, **did**, **get**, and **home** on the board, then show the children how to arrange words in alphabetical order.

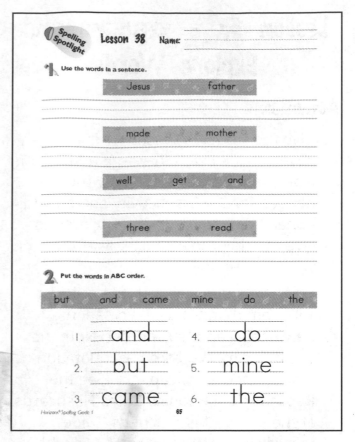

4. Ask the children to look at the word box for Activity 2. What word would come first if they wanted to put those words into ABC order? Write that word (**and**) on the line next to Number 1. What word would come next? Write the word. Continue this process until all words have been written in the correct alphabetical order.

Extended Activity:

Provide additional opportunities to arrange word cards or lists in alphabetical order.

Lesson 39 - Apply Understanding of Words in Writing

Teaching Tip:

For this page, children may work in teams or individually. Since the directions are very broad, some preparation for this activity is needed before the children are expected to write on their own. If children are having difficulty, write a class story using the review words and have the children copy it.

Activities:

1. Give the students Lesson 39. Have the children review the words in the box and the Working Words you have chosen for this review.

2. Ask the children for ideas for stories that might be written using the review words. Put the ideas on the board. Pick one idea. Ask for sentences using review words that can be used to tell a story about the idea chosen.

3. Write a class story. Then, tell the children that they can write their own stories using a different idea. Allow them to work in pairs for this project. Ask them to circle each spelling words that they use.

4. Share stories. See how many spelling words each story used.

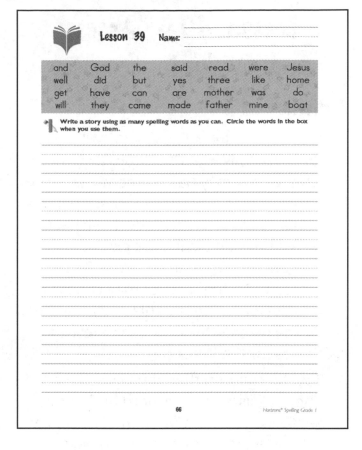

Lesson 40 - Assess and Evaluate Progress

Activities:

1. Give the students Lesson 40. Tell the children that this is a "Check-up" page to see what words they have remembered from previous weeks. [Note: Teachers/parents of home schoolers may decide what will be assessed. If a child did exceptionally well on the "What do you know?" pre-assessment, the teacher may choose not to test words already known by the child. Or the teacher may choose to test all Words for the Week.]

2. Tell the children that you will say a word. They will listen to the word and to the sentence you will give them. Then, they will write the word on the line next to the numbers. [Lines are given for the weekly words, but make sure to also check the Working Words for the week.]

3. Say the word. Repeat it in the context of a sentence. Repeat the word.

4. The children write the word dictated in the **Test** column.

5. The process is repeated until all words have been tested.

6. The teacher may correct in class by writing the words on the board and having the children compare or "self-correct" their work. Or the teacher may correct each child's work individually.

7. The teacher then uses the **Correction** column to write any corrections for words misspelled.

8. In the **Practice** column, the child copies the correct spelling of any words missed.

Check-up Time Lesson 40 Name:

Write the words your teacher reads.

1. ___ 13. ___ 25. ___
2. ___ 14. ___ 26. ___
3. ___ 15. ___ 27. ___
4. ___ 16. ___ 28. ___
5. ___ 17. ___
6. ___ 18. ___
7. ___ 19. ___
8. ___ 20. ___
9. ___ 21. ___
10. ___ 22. ___
11. ___ 23. ___
12. ___ 24. ___

Horizons Spelling Grade 1   67

9. The second side of the page can be used for retesting, for testing additional sight or "Working Words" added for the week, and for additional practice.

Extended Activity:

Review any words missed.

Week 9

Lessons 41-45: Assess Child's Knowledge

Goal: To recognize and spell words with the long ū sound, and with the /**ks**/ sound of **x**.

Review Rule: When a word or syllable has two vowels, the first vowel is usually long and the second vowel is usually silent—**rule, blue**.

Introduce Rule: When **x** comes at the end of a word, it is usually pronounced "**ks**." Example: **box**, **fox**.

What Do You Know?

Give the students the What do you know? page for Lessons 41-45. Tell them that this page will be used to see what they already know about the Words for the Week. Ask them to listen carefully to each word as you say it, repeat it in a sentence, and say it once again. Follow the procedures for this page as described in the *Introduction* at the beginning of this Teacher's Guide.

Ask the children to write their Working Words for the week in the word box and on their own paper.

Show the children how to write their Working Words in the appropriate section at the back of their *Spelling Dictionary*.

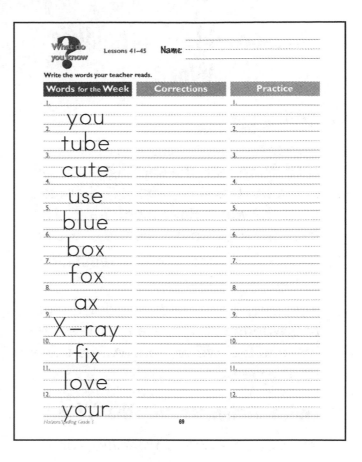

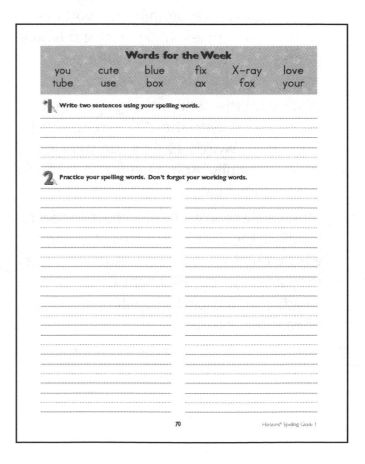

Lesson 41 - Introduce Words

Activities:

1. Give the students Lesson 41. Ask the children to read the spelling word printed on the first line (**box**). Ask them to trace the word. Have them draw a line from the word to the picture of the box.

2. Repeat the process for the remaining five words and pictures.

3. In Activity 2, the children will write the two Working Words given in the word box and the two Working Words chosen for the week.

Extended Activities for the Week:

1. Reproducible *Week 9 Worksheet* for in-class or take-home use.

   Begin building recognition by working with word families. Make a long $\bar{u}$ family page which is divided into different ways to spell the long $\bar{u}$ sound.

   Work with the children, or instruct parents to work with the children, to identify as many words as they can think of for each family. Add page for the different sounds of **x**.

2. Make a class word family chart for each family listed on the worksheet. Hang where children can see it. Add words as they are learned. Highlight or check off words that are part of spelling lessons or reading lessons.

3. Write sentences with the Working Words chosen for the week.

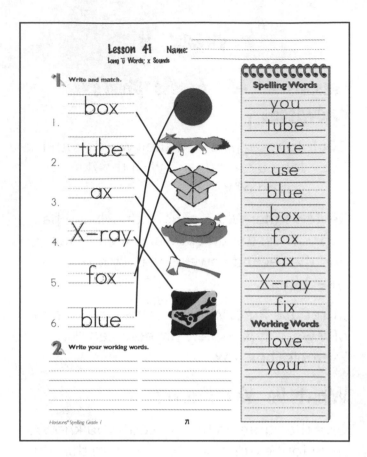

Lesson 42 - Examine and Explore Words

Teaching Tip:

Review spelling words, Working Words, and rules for the week.

Activities:

1. Give the students Lesson 42. Using the word box given for Activity 2, have the children study the shapes of the spelling words for this week.

2. Discuss with them the different ways to spell the long ū sound.

3. Have them find the words that will be written under each heading in the first activity. Write the words in the shape boxes.
   NOTE: Explain to the children that although the word **blue** does not exactly follow the pattern **_u_e**, the two vowels together still make the long **u** sound with the **e** being silent.

4. Read the directions for Activity 2. Read the words for the children or ask them to read them if they are able. Ask them to find a spelling word to rhyme with each of the words listed. Have them write the spelling word that rhymes next to the word.

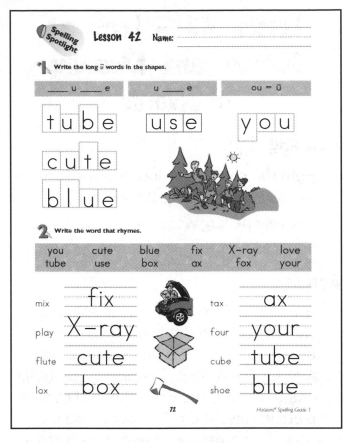

Extended Activities:

1. Continue work on word families.

2. Work with students who have difficulty hearing rhymes.

Lesson 43 - Look at Context and Meaning of Words

Teaching Tips:

1. Help the children to locate their spelling words in the *Spelling Dictionary*.
2. Review spelling words, Working Words, and rules for the week.

Activities:

1. Give the students Lesson 43. Ask the children to read the two words listed at the beginning of the first sentence in Activity 1. Ask them to read the sentence and to choose the word that will complete it. Have them first circle and then copy the correct word into the sentence. Repeat this process for the remaining sentences. Allow those children who are able to work independently.

2. Read the Bible verse to the children. Have the children read it with you. Copy the verse onto the lines provided.

Extended Activities:

1. Ask the children to give examples of ways in which they show love for others. Make a chart or collage of things that show love for others and write the Bible verse across the top of the chart

2. Add words from the Bible verse to appropriate word family charts.

Lesson 44 - Apply Understanding of Words in Writing

Teaching Tip:

Review spelling words, Working Words, and rules.

Activities:

1. Give the students Lesson 44. Have spelling word list, *Spelling Dictionary*, and word family pages available to help children in this activity.

2. Write the words: **I love...** on the board. Ask the children to name things that they love. List these on the board. Ask the children to tell why they love someone or something. Instruct children to write about someone or something that they love. When they have finished, have them draw a picture to accompany their stories.

3. Share stories and pictures with the class.

Lesson 44   Name: _____

1 Write about it.

I love _____

2 Draw a picture.

74   Horizons® Spelling Grade 1

Lesson 45 - Assess and Evaluate Progress

Activities:

1. Give the students Lesson 45. Tell the children that this is a "Check-up" page to see what they have learned during the week. [Note: Teachers/parents of home schoolers may decide what will be assessed. If a child did exceptionally well on the "What do you know?" pre-assessment, the teacher may choose not to test words already known by the child. Or the teacher may choose to test all Words for the Week.]

2. Tell the children that you will say a word. They will listen to the word and to the sentence you will give them. Then, they will write the word on the line next to the numbers. [Lines are given for the weekly words, but make sure to also check the Working Words for the week.]

3. Say the word. Repeat it in the context of a sentence. Repeat the word.

4. The children write the word dictated in the **Test** column.

5. The process is repeated until all words have been tested.

6. The teacher may correct in class by writing the words on the board and having the children compare or "self-correct" their work. Or the teacher may correct each child's work individually.

7. The teacher then uses the **Correction** column to write any corrections for words misspelled.

8. In the **Practice** column, the child copies the correct spelling of any words missed.

9. The second side of the page can be used for retesting, for testing additional sight or "Working Words" added for the week, and for additional practice.

Extended Activity:

Review any words missed.

Week 10

Lessons 46-50: Assess Child's Knowledge

Goals: To recognize, spell, and understand contractions; to spell words ending in double letters.

Introduce Rule: Contraction: short way to write two words as one. When the two words are put together, one or more letters are left out. A sign called an apostrophe (') is used to show where the letters were left out. (See the **Reproducible Phonics Rules Flashcards** at the end of this Teacher's Guide.)

What Do You Know?

Give the students the What do you know? page for Lessons 46-50. Tell them that this page will be used to see what they already know about the Words for the Week. Ask them to listen carefully to each word as you say it, repeat it in a sentence, and say it once again. Follow the procedures for this page as described in the *Introduction* at the beginning of this Teacher's Guide.

Ask the children to write their Working Words for the week in the word box and on their own paper.

Show the children how to write their Working Words in the appropriate section at the back of their *Spelling Dictionary*.

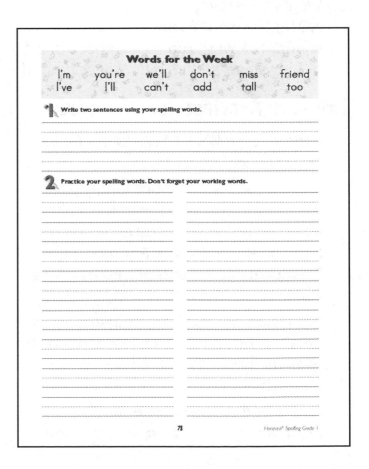

Lesson 46 - Introduce Words

Activities:

1. Give the students Lesson 46. Write the words **I am** on the board. Underneath these words, write the contraction **I'm**. Tell the children that in this spelling lesson, they will be learning some shortcuts that we use to combine words when we speak. Go to the first exercise on the page. The children will see **I am** next to Number 1. Have them write the contraction **I'm** on the line provided.

2. Continue introducing the remaining contractions in the same manner. Use the rule cards or post them around the room to assist children who have difficulty.

3. Ask the children to write their Working Words for Activity 2.
   NOTE: The word **friend** has a short **ĕ** sound. The word **too** has neither a short or long vowel sound, but a special sound.

Extended Activities for the Week:

1. Reproducible *Week 10 Worksheet* for in-class or take-home use.

   Make a contraction word family page for each of the contractions in this unit: **not/n't**; **am/'m**; **will/'ll**; **are/'re**; **have/'ve** (See the **Reproducible Phonics Rules Flashcards** at the end of this Teacher's Guide.)

   Work with the children, or instruct parents to work with the children, to identify as many words as they can think of for each family.

   Add **friend** to the short **ĕ** family page. Begin a page for the **oo** sound in **too**.

2. Make a class word family chart for each family listed on the worksheet. Hang where children can see it. Add words as they are learned. Highlight or check off words that are part of spelling lessons or reading lessons.

3. Write sentences with the Working Words chosen for the week.

Lesson 47 - Examine and Explore Words

Teaching Tip:

Review spelling words, Working Words, and rule.

Activities:

1. Give the students Lesson 47. Review the spelling words in the word box. Ask the children to select a spelling word from the box to complete each sentence in the first activity.

2. Do the first sentence together. If children are able, allow them to complete independently. Check together.

3. Read the directions for Activity 2 with the children. Allow them to work on this independently as they are able. Check together.

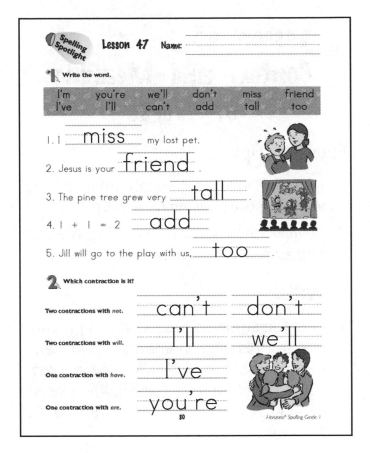

Extended Activities:

1. Continue work with contractions for students having difficulty.

2. Begin word family pages for words ending in double letters: __ll, __dd, __ss.

Lesson 48 - Look at Context and Meaning of Words

Teaching Tips:

1. Help the children to locate their spelling words in the *Spelling Dictionary*.
2. Review spelling words, Working Words, and rules for the week.

Activities:

1. Give the students Lesson 48. As preparation for this page, prepare a set of "sentence cards" for each child. These cards can be duplicated, cut apart, and placed in an envelope. Use simple sentences of five words or less.

   Examples: John had a ball.
   The box was full.
   I'll come home soon.

   Cut each sentence apart and keep it separate from the others. Give these sentence cards to the children and ask them to lay the individual cards out on their desks/tables. Ask the children to arrange the cards so that they form a sentence. Help children as needed. Repeat this process until the children can quickly arrange simple sentences with ease.

2. Ask the children to look at the first line of words in Activity 1. Tell them that these words are a mixed-up sentence. Ask them to study the words so that they can arrange them into a real sentence. Have them look for clues: a word with a capital letter to begin the sentence. When the children have solved the first sentence, **I've got a red ball.** Have them write it on the line provided.
   NOTE: If children have difficulty, write the

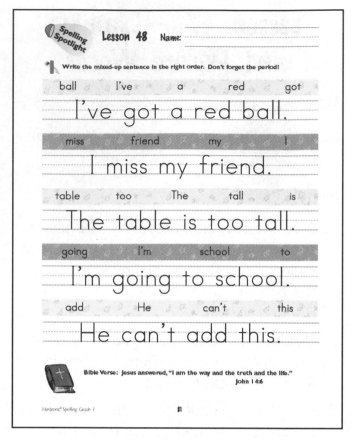

sentences for this activity on individual cards so the children can actually move the words around to make the sentence.

3. Repeat this process for the remaining four scrambled sentences on the page.

4. Read the Bible verse to the children. Have them read it with you. Explain to them that in serious writing, like the Bible, we do not use contractions. We would not say, "I'm the way,..." Talk about the verse. How does Jesus show us the way to heaven? What truth does He teach us? What life is He talking about?

5. Have the children write the verse on good paper and decorate it with a special border or picture.

Extended Activities:

1. Continue practice with scrambled sentences if children are having difficulty.

2. Complete work on any word family pages begun this week.

Horizons Spelling Grade 1

Lesson 49 - Apply Understanding of Words in Writing

Teaching Tip:

Review spelling words, Working Words, and rule for the week.

Activities:

1. Give the students Lesson 49. Have spelling words, Working Words for the week and *Spelling Dictionary* at hand, as well as any other word family charts or rule charts that may be needed.

2. Read the directions with the children. Ask them to think carefully about a good friend. Have them draw a picture of their friend in the space provided.

3. Spend some time talking about their friends. Why are they good friends? What do they do to show they are friends? What are their names? What do they look like? Write some of the descriptive words used by the children on the board to assist them in their writing.

4. Ask the children to use the lines given to write about the friend they drew in the picture box.

5. Share stories with the class.

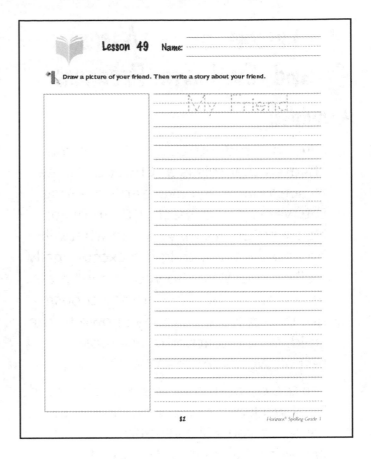

Lesson 50 - Assess and Evaluate Progress

Activities:

1. Give the students Lesson 50. Tell the children that this is a "Check-up" page to see what they have learned during the week. [Note: Teachers/parents of home schoolers may decide what will be assessed. If a child did exceptionally well on the "What do you know?" pre-assessment, the teacher may choose not to test words already known by the child. Or the teacher may choose to test all Words for the Week.]

2. Tell the children that you will say a word. They will listen to the word and to the sentence you will give them. Then, they will write the word on the line next to the numbers. [Lines are given for the weekly words, but make sure to also check the Working Words for the week.]

3. Say the word. Repeat it in the context of a sentence. Repeat the word.

4. The children write the word dictated in the **Test** column.

5. The process is repeated until all words have been tested.

6. The teacher may correct in class by writing the words on the board and having the children compare or "self-correct" their work. Or the teacher may correct each child's work individually.

7. The teacher then uses the **Correction** column to write any corrections for words misspelled.

8. In the **Practice** column, the child copies the correct spelling of any words missed.

9. The second side of the page can be used for retesting, for testing additional sight or "Working Words" added for the week, and for additional practice.

Extended Activity:

Review any words missed.

Week 11

Lessons 51-55: Assess Child's Knowledge

Goal: To recognize and spell plural words ending in **-s** and **-es**.

Rule: A word is plural if it means more than one. Example: **trucks**, **cars**, **plates**, **things**.

Rule: When a word ends in **ss**, **ch**, **sh**, or **x**, usually add **es** at the end to make the word plural.

What Do You Know?

Give the students the What do you know? page for Lessons 51-55. Tell them that this page will be used to see what they already know about the Words for the Week. Ask them to listen carefully to each word as you say it, repeat it in a sentence, and say it once again. Follow the procedures for this page as described in the *Introduction* at the beginning of this Teacher's Guide.

Ask the children to write their Working Words for the week in the word box and on their own paper.

Show the children how to write their Working Words in the appropriate section at the back of their *Spelling Dictionary*.

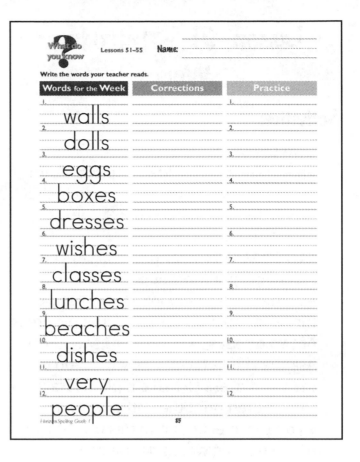

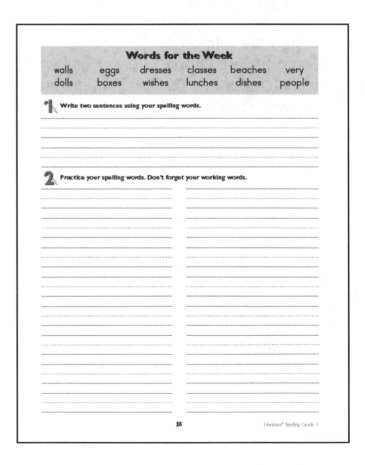

Lesson 51 - Introduce Words

Activities:

1. Give the students Lesson 51. Spend time reviewing the idea of plurals with the children. Use things at hand in the room: pencils, papers, books, desks, tables, and so on.

   NOTE: One irregular plural occurs on this page: **person/people**.

   Ask the children to look at the first picture and word on the page. The picture is of two dresses, but the word says **dress**. Ask the children what they must do to the word **dress** to make it plural. Have the children print the entire word **dress-es** on the line. Continue this process for the remaining words on the page.

2. Have the children take note of which plurals add **–s** and which add **–es**. Review the rule card. (See the **Reproducible Phonics Rules Flashcards** at the end of this Teacher's Guide dealing with plurals.)

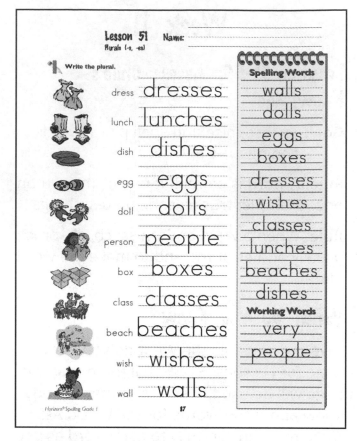

Extended Activities for the Week:

1. Reproducible *Week 11 Worksheet* for in-class or take-home use.

   Begin building recognition by working with word families. Make a family page for plurals ending in **–s** and one for plurals ending in **–es**.

   Work with the children, or instruct parents to work with the children, to identify as many words as they can think of for each family.

2. Make a class word family chart for each family listed on the worksheet. Hang where children can see it. Add words as they are learned. Highlight or check off words that are part of spelling lessons or reading lessons.

3. Write sentences with the Working Words chosen for the week.

Lesson 52 - Examine and Explore Words

Teaching Tip:

Review spelling words, Working Words, and rule for plurals.

Activities:

1. Give the students Lesson 52. Review the spelling words in the purple word box. Read the directions with the children. Help them with the first few, and then allow them to continue independently if they are able. Check together.

2. In Activity 2, tell the children that they will use the words in the green box to complete the sentences. Do the first sentence together. Allow the children to complete the activity. Check together.

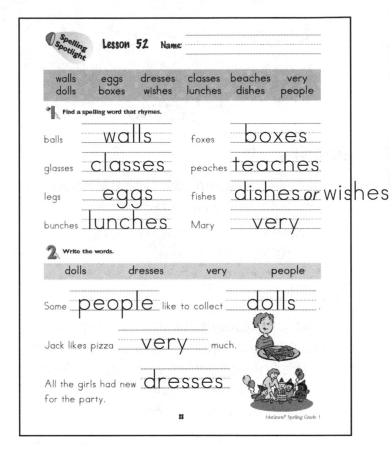

Extended Activity:

Continue work on plural word families.

Lesson 53 - Look at Context and Meaning of Words

Teaching Tips:

1. Help the children to locate their spelling words in the *Spelling Dictionary*.
2. Review spelling words, Working Words, and rules for the week.

Activities:

1. Give the students Lesson 53. Tell the children that spelling words are hidden in the lines of letters given in the first activity. The pictures on the side are clues to the hidden words.

2. Ask the children to look at the first line and find the hidden spelling word (**boxes**). Ask them to circle the word. Have them print the word on the line and then draw a line to the picture of the boxes. Repeat this process for the remaining hidden words or allow children to complete independently and check together.

3. Read the directions for Activity 2. Do the first sentence together by selecting the correct word, circling it, and writing it on the line. Complete activity and check.

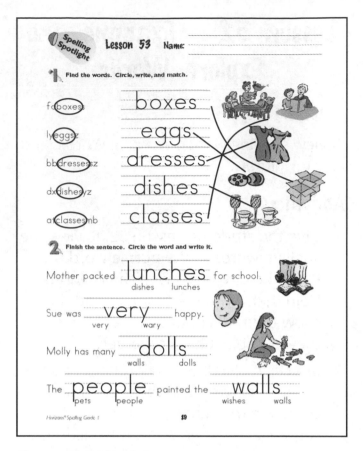

Extended Activity:

In preparation for the writing activity in Lesson 54, read Matthew 14:13–21. Talk about what Jesus did.

Lesson 54 - Apply Understanding of Words in Writing

Teaching Tip:

Review spelling words, Working Words, and rule for plurals.

Activities:

1. Give the students Lesson 54. Recall the story from Matthew read to the children. Read again, if needed. Ask the children to retell the story in their own words. What do they remember?

2. Tell the children that now they will have a chance to write the main part of the story in their own words. Encourage them to use spelling words, Working Words, and their *Spelling Dictionary* to look for words they do not remember how to spell.

3. Share stories or act out story with the class.

Lesson 54   Name:

Write a story that tells what Jesus did with five loaves and two fishes.

Jesus Feeds the People

90   Horizons® Spelling Grade 1

Lesson 55 - Assess and Evaluate Progress

Activities:

1. Give the students Lesson 55. Tell the children that this is a "Check-up" page to see what they have learned during the week. [Note: Teachers/parents of home schoolers may decide what will be assessed. If a child did exceptionally well on the "What do you know?" pre-assessment, the teacher may choose not to test words already known by the child. Or the teacher may choose to test all Words for the Week.]

2. Tell the children that you will say a word. They will listen to the word and to the sentence you will give them. Then, they will write the word on the line next to the numbers. [Lines are given for the weekly words, but make sure to also check the Working Words for the week.]

3. Say the word. Repeat it in the context of a sentence. Repeat the word.

4. The children write the word dictated in the **Test** column.

5. The process is repeated until all words have been tested.

6. The teacher may correct in class by writing the words on the board and having the children compare or "self-correct" their work. Or the teacher may correct each child's work individually.

7. The teacher then uses the **Correction** column to write any corrections for words misspelled.

8. In the **Practice** column, the child copies the correct spelling of any words missed.

9. The second side of the page can be used for retesting, for testing additional sight or "Working Words" added for the week, and for additional practice.

Extended Activity:

Review any words missed.

Week 12

Lessons 56-60: Assess Child's Knowledge

Goal: To recognize and spell words used in comparisons ending with the suffixes –er and –est.

Rule: A suffix is an ending that is added to a word. Many words do not have to have the spelling changed before the suffix is added. Examples: **jumped**, **locked**, **dresses**.

Rule: The suffix –er can be used to compare two things. Examples: **near/nearer**.

Rule: The suffix –er sometimes means "a person who." Example: Someone who works is a worker. Someone who sings is a singer.

Rule: The suffix –est is used to compare more than two things. Examples: **tall/tallest**, **short/shortest**. Sue is shorter than her sister. (comparing two things) She is the shortest in her family (Comparing more than two things).

Rule: When a words ends in **y** after a consonant, change the **y** to **i** before adding –er to the end. Examples: **pretty/prettier**; **busy/busiest**.

Rule: When a words ends in **y** after a consonant, change the **y** to **i** before adding –est to the end. Examples: **pretty/prettiest**; **lonely/loneliest**.

What Do You Know?

Give the students the What do you know? page for Lessons 56-60. Tell them that this page will be used to see what they already know about the Words for the Week. Ask them to listen carefully to each word as you say it, repeat it in a sentence, and say it once again. Follow the procedures for this page as described in the *Introduction* at the beginning of this Teacher's Guide.

Ask the children to write their Working Words for the week in the word box and on their own paper.

Horizons Spelling Grade 1

Show the children how to write their Working Words in the appropriate section at the back of their *Spelling Dictionary*.

Lesson 56 - Introduce Words

Activities:

1. Give the students Lesson 56. Visually demonstrate some of the words in this lesson. Examples: Take a piece of yarn or string that is long. Cut a second piece that is longer than the first and a third that is the longest of the three. Find pictures of something moving fast. Find another picture of something that moves faster than the first and a third that shows the fastest of the three. Point to a tree that reaches high into the sky. Point to a building or a bird that is flying higher than the tree. Point to the clouds or the sun that is highest in the sky. Ask the children for examples of things that can be compared.

2. Point out the formation of comparison words: adding –**er** when comparing two things; adding –**est** when comparing three or more.

3. Read the directions for the first activity with the children and complete.

4. As the children write their Working Words in Activity 2, point out the fact that some words do NOT add –**er** and –**est** to compare. Use examples to demonstrate **some, more, most.**

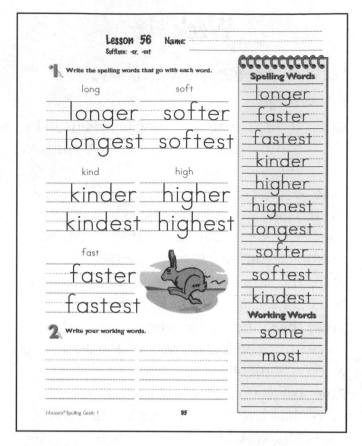

Extended Activities for the Week:

1. Reproducible *Week 12 Worksheet* for in-class or take-home use.

   Make a word family page to show comparisons: **long**, **longer**, **longest**; **soft**, **softer**, **softest**, and so on.

   Work with the children, or instruct parents to work with the children, to identify as many words as they can think of for each family.

2. Make a class word family chart for each family listed on the worksheet. Hang where children can see it. Add words as they are learned. Highlight or check off words that are part of spelling lessons or reading lessons.

3. Write sentences with the Working Words chosen for the week.

Horizons Spelling Grade 1

Lesson 57 – Examine and Explore Words

Teaching Tip:

Review rules, spelling words and Working Words.

Activities:

1. Give the students Lesson 57.
   NOTE: If a child has any visual difficulties with word search puzzles, provide aids to help isolate words in the box.

2. Review the words in the box with the children. Tell them that these words are hidden in the puzzle box. Ask them to find each word and circle it.

3. Sentences for the Working Words chosen for the week can be written as a class or individually.

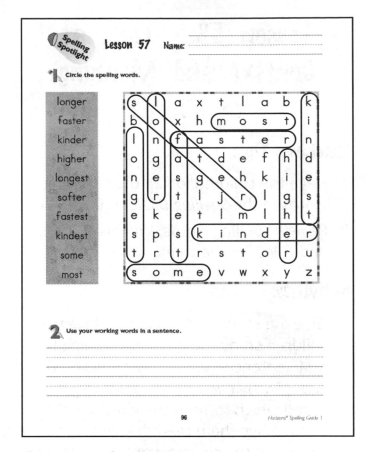

Extended Activity:

If children have problems understanding comparisons, provide additional activities to reinforce the concepts.

Lesson 58 - Look at Context and Meaning of Words

Teaching Tips:

1. Have the children locate their spelling words in the *Spelling Dictionary*.
2. Review spelling words, Working Words, and rules for the week.

Activities:

1. Give the students Lesson 58. Have the children study the picture following the first sentence. How many things do they see? (**Two**). If two things are being compared which form of the word will they need? Have them read the sentence supplying the correct word. Ask them to circle the correct word. Repeat this process for the remaining sentences.

2. Read the Bible verse to the children. Have them read it with you. Ask them where this verse fits in the life of Jesus. Reread the section of Luke if they do not remember. Ask them which word in the verse is a spelling word.

3. Have the children write the verse on special paper and illustrate it.

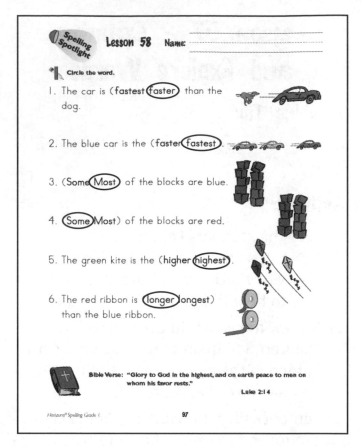

Extended Activity:

Have the children share their Bible verse, story, and illustration with family and friends.

Lesson 59 - Apply Understanding of Words in Writing

Teaching Tip:

Review comparisons, spelling words, Working Words, and rules.

Activities:

1. Give the students Lesson 59. Talk about things that are soft. Ask the children to think of the softest thing they have at home. Tell them they will write a sentence about that thing and draw a picture of it in the box.

2. Talk about things that kind people do for others. Ask the children to think of the kindest person they know. Have them write a short description of the kindest person they know and draw a picture.

3. Share sentences and pictures with the class.

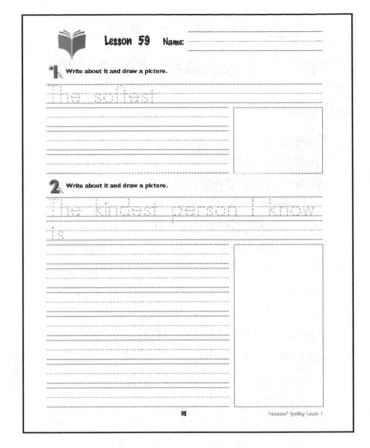

Lesson 60 - Assess and Evaluate Progress

Activities:

1. Give the students Lesson 60. Tell the children that this is a "Check-up" page to see what they have learned during the week. [Note: Teachers/parents of home schoolers may decide what will be assessed. If a child did exceptionally well on the "What do you know?" pre-assessment, the teacher may choose not to test words already known by the child. Or the teacher may choose to test all Words for the Week.]

2. Tell the children that you will say a word. They will listen to the word and to the sentence you will give them. Then, they will write the word on the line next to the numbers. [Lines are given for the weekly words, but make sure to also check the Working Words for the week.]

3. Say the word. Repeat it in the context of a sentence. Repeat the word.

4. The children write the word dictated in the **Test** column.

5. The process is repeated until all words have been tested.

6. The teacher may correct in class by writing the words on the board and having the children compare or "self-correct" their work. Or the teacher may correct each child's work individually.

7. The teacher then uses the **Correction** column to write any corrections for words misspelled.

8. In the **Practice** column, the child copies the correct spelling of any words missed.

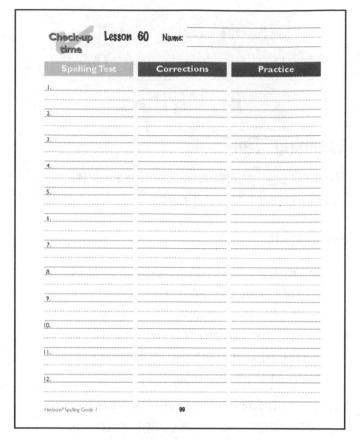

9. The second side of the page can be used for retesting, for testing additional sight or "Working Words" added for the week, and for additional practice.

Extended Activity:

Review any words missed.

Week 13

Lessons 61-65: Assess Child's Knowledge

Goal: To recognize and learn to spell words with the suffixes: **–ful**, **–ing**, and **–ness**.

Rule: A suffix is an ending that is added to a word to make a new word. Usually when the suffixes **–ful**, **–ly**, **–less** or **–ness** are added, the spelling of the base word does not change. Examples: **painful**, **sadness**, **hopeless**, **quickly**.

Rule: Base words are words that do not have a prefix (beginning) or suffix (ending) added to them.

What Do You Know?

Give the students the What do you know? page for Lessons 61-65. Tell them that this page will be used to see what they already know about the Words for the Week. Ask them to listen carefully to each word as you say it, repeat it in a sentence, and say it once again. Follow the procedures for this page as described in the *Introduction* at the beginning of this Teacher's Guide.

Ask the children to write their Working Words for the week in the box and on their own paper.

Show the children how to write their Working Words in the appropriate section at the back of their *Spelling Dictionary*.

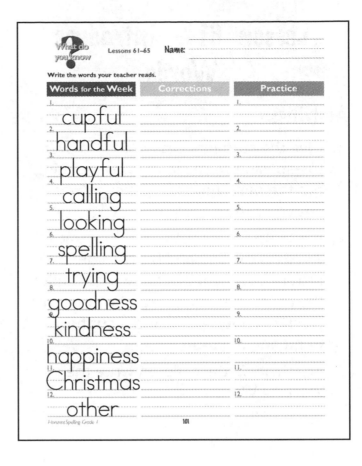

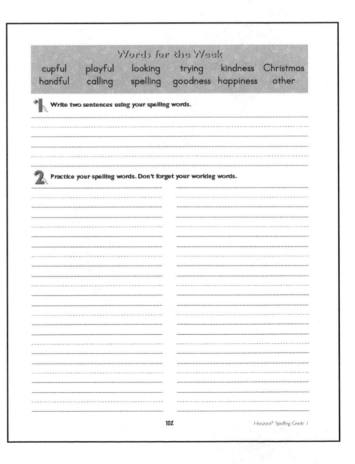

Lesson 61 - Introduce Words

Activities:

1. Give the students Lesson 61. Go over the spelling words in the box, pointing out the base words and the suffixes added to the base words.

2. In the first activity, the children trace the word on the line and draw a line to the picture that matches the word. Caution the children to look carefully to distinguish between a **cup** and a **cupful**, a **hand** and a **handful**.

3. In Activity 2, the children write their Working Words.

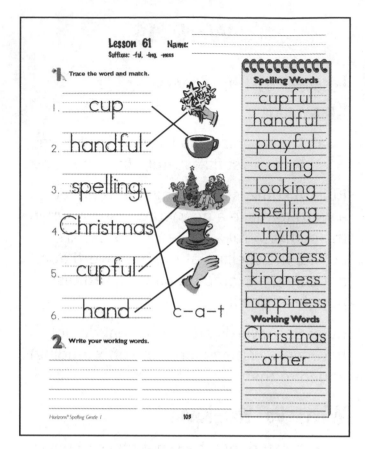

Extended Activities for the Week:

1. Reproducible *Week 13 Worksheet* for in-class or take-home use.

2. Make a class word family chart for the words and suffixes used in this lesson. Hang where children can see it. Add words as they are learned. Highlight or check off words that are part of spelling lessons or reading lessons.

3. Write sentences with the Working Words chosen for the week.

Lesson 62 - Examine and Explore Words

Teaching Tip:

Review rule, spelling words and Working Words.

Activities:

1. Give the students Lesson 62. This page gives the children practice in adding a suffix to a base word to form a new word. Make special note of the final word **happy/happiness**. Demonstrate the formation of this word for the children.

2. Instruct the children to write the complete word on the line provided.

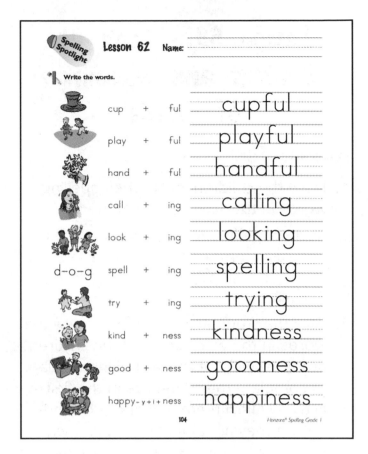

Horizons Spelling Grade 1

Lesson 63 - Look at Context and Meaning of Words

Teaching Tips:

1. Have the children locate their spelling words in the *Spelling Dictionary*.
2. Review spelling words, Working Words, and rules for the week.

Activities:

1. Give the students Lesson 63. Review the words in the word box. Tell the children that they will use these spelling words to complete the sentences in the first activity. Allow them to work independently if they are able. Check together.

2. Sentences for the Working Words chosen for the week may be written together as a class and copied in the book or written independently.

3. Look at the pictures that accompany the Bible verse. Talk about them. Read the Bible verse. Have the children read it with you. Review the Christmas story with the children.

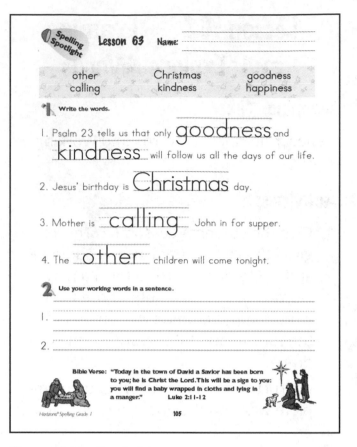

Extended Activity:

Have the children divide the verse into sections and make a Christmas booklet illustrating each part of the verse.

Lesson 64 - Apply Understanding of Words in Writing

Teaching Tip:

Review words that are related to Christmas, spelling words, Working Words, and rules.

Activities:

1. Give the students Lesson 64. Write the words **happiness**, **kindness**, and **goodness** on the board. Ask the children what those words mean to them. Ask them how those words are expressed at Christmas time.

2. Help them to plan a Christmas story that talks about those three concepts. They may draw the picture for the story before or after they write their stories.

3. Share stories and pictures with class.

Lesson 64   Name:

Christmas is a time of *happiness*, *kindness*, and *goodness*. Draw a picture and write a Christmas story using these words.

cupful
handful
playful
calling
looking
spelling
trying
goodness
kindness
happiness
Christmas
other

106   *Horizons® Spelling Grade 1*

Lesson 65 - Assess and Evaluate Progress

Activities:

1. Give the students Lesson 65. Tell the children that this is a "Check-up" page to see what they have learned during the week. [Note: Teachers/parents of home schoolers may decide what will be assessed. If a child did exceptionally well on the "What do you know?" pre-assessment, the teacher may choose not to test words already known by the child. Or the teacher may choose to test all Words for the Week.]

2. Tell the children that you will say a word. They will listen to the word and to the sentence you will give them. Then, they will write the word on the line next to the numbers. [Lines are given for the weekly words, but make sure to also check the Working Words for the week.]

3. Say the word. Repeat it in the context of a sentence. Repeat the word.

4. The children write the word dictated in the **Test** column.

5. The process is repeated until all words have been tested.

6. The teacher may correct in class by writing the words on the board and having the children compare or "self-correct" their work. Or the teacher may correct each child's work individually.

7. The teacher then uses the **Correction** column to write any corrections for words misspelled.

8. In the **Practice** column, the child copies the correct spelling of any words missed.

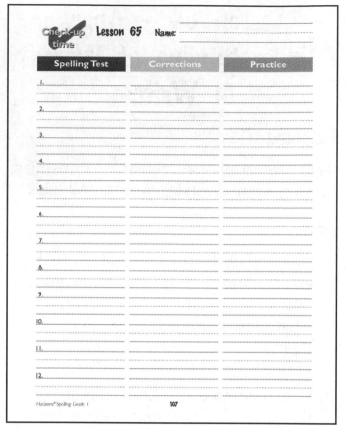

9. The second side of the page can be used for retesting, for testing additional sight or "Working Words" added for the week, and for additional practice.

Extended Activity:

Review any words missed.

Week 14

Lessons 66-70: Assess Child's Knowledge

Goals: To recognize and spell words with silent letters: **igh**, **mb**, **ck**, **kn**, **gn**, **gn**, **wr**, and **wh**; to spell two common abbreviated words.

Rule: In consonant digraph **kn** k is silent and **n** is pronounced.

Rule: In consonant digraph **gn** the **g** is silent and the **n** is pronounced. Examples: **sign**, **align**.

Rule: In consonant digraph **ck** the **c** and the **k** go together to make the **k** sound. Examples: **clock**, **back**.

Rule: In consonant digraph **wr** the **w** is silent and the **r** is pronounced. Example: **write**, **wrong**.

Rule: In consonant digraph **wh** the **wh** makes the **w** sound. Example: **what**, **when**.

Rule: In consonant digraph **mb** the **b** is silent and the **m** is pronounced. Example: **comb**.

NOTE: From this week forward, two additional spelling words have been added to the list, making a total of 14 spelling words plus two choice Working Words.

What Do You Know?

Give the students the What do you know? page for Lessons 66-70. Tell them that this page will be used to see what they already know about the Words for the Week. Ask them to listen carefully to each word as you say it, repeat it in a sentence, and say it once again. Follow the procedures for this page as described in the *Introduction* at the beginning of this Teacher's Guide.

Ask the children to write their Working Words for the week on their own paper.

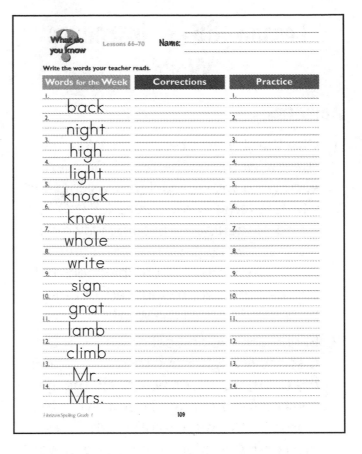

Show the children how to write their Working Words in the appropriate section at the back of their *Spelling Dictionary*.

Lesson 66 - Introduce Words

Activities:

1. Give the students Lesson 66. Write the spelling words on the board. Go over each word with the children, asking them which letter(s) in each word CANNOT be heard. Underline, or in some way mark those letters. Explain that sometimes words have letters or combinations of letters that are not pronounced, but must be learned to spell the word correctly.

2. Begin with the first set of words in the first activity: **igh**. Have the children identify the three words which use the **igh** spelling for the long **ī** sound. Write the words (**night**, **high**, **light**) on the lines provided. Complete each group of words in the same manner, noting the sound each letter group represents: **kn = n; mb = m; gn = n; ck = k; wr = r; wh = w.**

3. Put the abbreviations **Mr.** and **Mrs.** on the board. Explain to the children that sometimes we shorten words that are used in titles or street names. Have them think of other examples: **St.**, **Ave.**, **Rd.**, etc. Also note that each state has an abbreviation, and review the abbreviation for the state in which they live.

4. Ask the children to complete Activity 2 by writing their four Working Words for the week.

Extended Activities for the Week:

1. Reproducible *Week 14 Worksheet* for in-class or take-home use. Build a silent letter word family page. Include all the silent letter combinations for this unit: **igh**, **kn**, **mb**, **gn**, **ck**, **wr**, **wh**. Work with the children, or instruct parents to work with the children, to identify as many words as they can think of for each family.

Begin an abbreviation page listing both the abbreviations they know and the complete word for the abbreviation. Example: **St. = Street, AZ = Arizona**, etc.

2. Make a class word family chart for each family listed on the worksheet. Hang where children can see it. Add words as they are learned. Highlight or check off words that are part of spelling lessons or reading lessons.

3. Write sentences with the Working Words chosen for the week.

Lesson 67 - Examine and Explore Words

Teaching Tips:

1. Review spelling words, Working Words and rules for the week.
2. Have *Spelling Dictionary* available.

Activities:

1. Give the students Lesson 67. Write the spelling words **know**, **lamb**, and **high** on the board. Have the children look at the first letter of each word. Ask them to help you put the words in ABC order as they would be found in their *Spelling Dictionary*.

2. Look at Activity 1. Ask the children to read the words in the blue box. Tell them that they will be putting these words into ABC order. Ask which word will be the first (**back**). Have them write that word on the line next to Number 1. Ask which word will come next (**climb**). Have them write the word next to Number 2. Continue until all six words are written in the correct ABC order.

3. In Activity 2, the children will learn where the two abbreviated spelling words come from. Read the two words with the children. Note the underlined letters in each. Have the children write the abbreviation. Don't forget the period after each.

4. In Activity 3, the children will cross out the letters they cannot hear in each word given. Write the first word, **back**, on the board. Ask the children which letter is silent (**c**). Draw an **x** or **/** through the letter **c**. Have the children do the

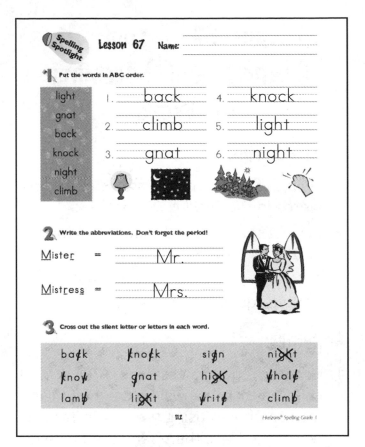

same in their books. Repeat the process for the remaining words, or allow those who are able to complete independently and check.

Extended Activity:

Add to word family charts.

Lesson 68 - Look at Context and Meaning of Words

Teaching Tips:

1. Help the children to locate their spelling words in the *Spelling Dictionary*.
2. Review spelling words, Working Words, and rules for the week.
3. Review writing of sentences: capitals, periods, question marks, etc.

Activities:

1. Give the students Lesson 68. Tell the children that they will be creating their own sentences using the words in each word box. Have them read the first two words: **lamb**, **climb**. Ask them for ideas, for sentences in which they could use both words. Write a sample sentence on the board. According to the level of the children, have them create their own sentences or use the one created by the class and write it on the line provided. Have the children complete the next two sentences independently. Check and share sentences with the class.

2. In Activity 2, the children will create two more sentences. Have them try to use all four Working Words in the sentences.

3. Read the Bible verse to the children and have them read it with you. Read the section from John in which the verse occurs. Talk about what "Lamb of God" means.

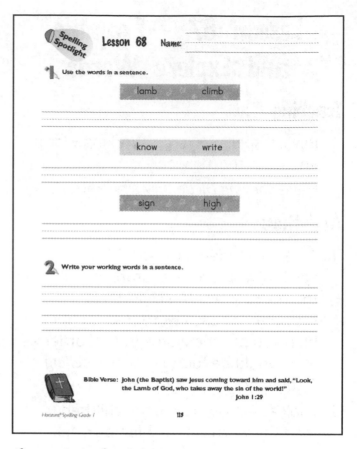

Extended Activities:

1. Have the children copy the Bible verse onto good paper. Ask them to add a few sentences of their own, thanking Jesus for being the "lamb" that has come to save us. Illustrate or decorate their pages.

2. Share drawings and sentences with the class.

Lesson 69 - Apply Understanding of Words in Writing

Teaching Tip:

Review spelling words, Working Words, rules, and word family charts.

Activities:

1. Give the students Lesson 69. Explain that in this activity the children can have some fun creating a "silly" story about a gnat that knocks over the light one night. Review the words. Discuss the picture. Have the children "brainstorm" some ideas.

2. Have the children write their stories. They may want to do a draft on practice paper first, then copy it into their books.

3. Help as needed. Encourage use of *Spelling Dictionary* and word family charts for help with the spelling of words not in this week's lesson.

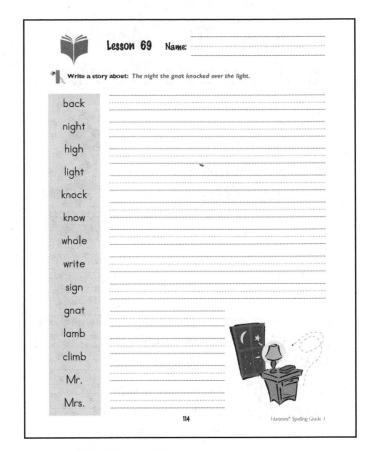

Extended Activity:

Share stories with the class.

Lesson 70 - Assess and Evaluate Progress

Activities:

1. Give the students Lesson 70. Tell the children that this is a "Check-up" page to see what they have learned during the week. [Note: Teachers/parents of home schoolers may decide what will be assessed. If a child did exceptionally well on the "What do you know?" pre-assessment, the teacher may choose not to test words already known by the child. Or the teacher may choose to test all Words for the Week.]

2. Tell the children that you will say a word. They will listen to the word and to the sentence you will give them. Then, they will write the word on the line next to the numbers. [Lines are given for the weekly words, but make sure to also check the Working Words for the week.]

3. Say the word. Repeat it in the context of a sentence. Repeat the word.

4. The children write the word dictated in the **Test** column.

5. The process is repeated until all words have been tested.

6. The teacher may correct in class by writing the words on the board and having the children compare or "self-correct" their work. Or the teacher may correct each child's work individually.

7. The teacher then uses the **Correction** column to write any corrections for words misspelled.

8. In the **Practice** column, the child copies the correct spelling of any words missed.

9. The second side of the page can be used for retesting, for testing additional sight or "Working Words" added for the week, and for additional practice.

Extended Activity:

Review any words missed.

Week 15

Lessons 71-75: Assess Child's Knowledge

Goal: To recognize and spell with the long and short **oo** sound and the three sounds of **ea**.

Rule: Vowel digraphs are two vowels put together in a word that make a long or short sound, or have a special sound all their own. The vowel digraph **oo** can stand for the vowel sound heard in **book**, or in **pool**. The vowel digraph **ea** can stand for the short **ĕ** sound heard in **head**. (See the **Reproducible Phonics Rules Flashcards** at the end of this Teacher's Guide for rules regarding vowel digraphs.)

What Do You Know?

Give the students the What do you know? page for Lessons 71-75. Tell them that this page will be used to see what they already know about the Words for the Week. Ask them to listen carefully to each word as you say it, repeat it in a sentence, and say it once again. Follow the procedures for this page as described in the *Introduction* at the beginning of this Teacher's Guide.

Ask the children to write their Working Words for the week in the word box and on their own paper.

Show the children how to write their Working Words in the appropriate section at the back of their *Spelling Dictionary*.

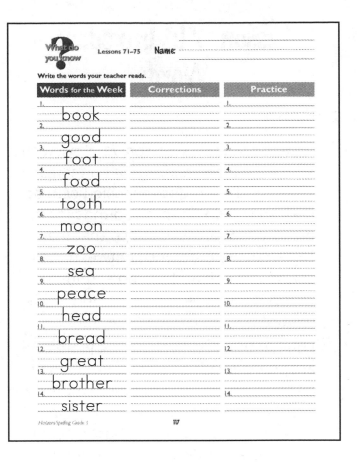

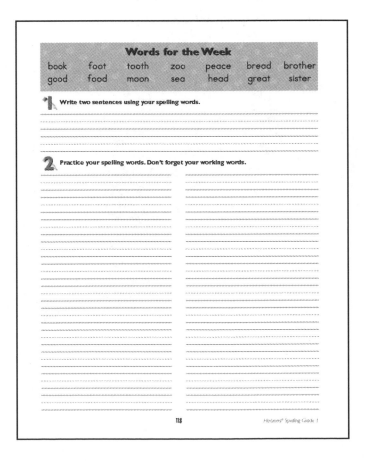

Lesson 71: Introduce Words

Activities:

1. Give the students Lesson 71. Review the words. Tell the children that although seven of the words are spelled with **oo**, they show two different sounds for the **oo**. Say the words aloud so that they can hear the difference between the **oo** sound in **book** and the **oo** sound in **moon**. Complete the words under the picture of the book and the moon.

2. Look at the next five spelling words. All are spelled with an **ea** combination of letters. Say the words aloud. Emphasize the difference in the sound of **ea** in **sea** (long ē sound), in **head** (short ĕ sound), and in **great** (long ā sound). Complete the words in the three **ea** sections.

3. Write Working Words.

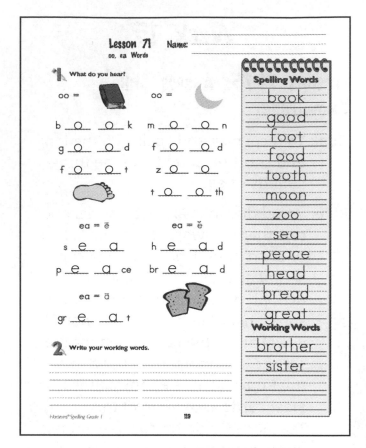

Extended Activities for the Week:

1. Reproducible *Week 15 Worksheet* for in-class or take-home use.

   Begin building recognition by working with word families. Make a word family page which is divided into different sounds for oo and ea. Work with the children, or instruct parents to work with the children, to identify as many words as they can think of for each family. Add to the "family names" word family page.

2. Make a class word family chart for each family listed on the worksheet. Hang where children can see it. Add words as they are learned. Highlight or check off words that are part of spelling lessons or reading lessons.

3. Write sentences with the Working Words chosen for the week.

Lesson 72 - Examine and Explore Words

Teaching Tip:

Review spelling words, Working Words, and rules.

Activities:

1. Give the students Lesson 72. Review the pictures and words with the children. Ask the children to select words from the purple word box and write them under the appropriate picture. Allow them to work independently.

2. Check.

Extended Activity:

Add to word family charts.

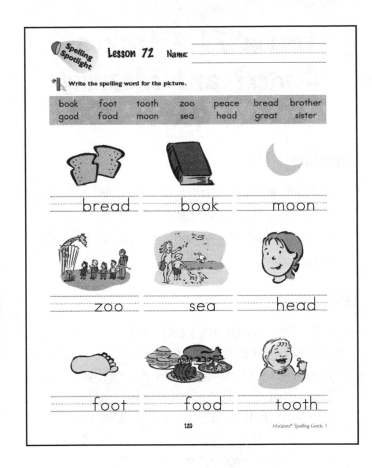

Lesson 73 - Look at Context and Meaning of Words

Teaching Tips:

1. Help the children to locate their spelling words in the *Spelling Dictionary*.
2. Review spelling words, Working Words, and rules for the week.

Activities:

1. Give the students Lesson 73. Review the concept of opposites as needed. Ask the children to find a spelling word that is the opposite for each of the words printed in the first activity. Write the words in the appropriate space. Check. NOTE: The word "**more**" is the correct answer to the opposite of "**less;**" however, **more** is not a spelling word. Explain to the students that this is a "bonus" answer to see if they understand the concept of opposites. The children should refer to the Words for the Week or the word list in the Activity 2 in completing the remainder of this Activity.

2. Children should be familiar with a crossword format by this stage, but if they are not, review how a crossword is done. Do Number 1 Across together. Check to see that the children have entered the word correctly. Proceed, either completing the numbers Across first, OR alternating numbers in order, regardless of whether they go across or down.

Extended Activities:

1. Provide additional crossword practice as needed.
2. Have children attempt to create their own short crossword puzzles.

Lesson 74 - Apply Understanding of Words in Writing

Teaching Tip:

Review spelling words, Working Words, word family charts, and rules.

Activities:

1. Give the students Lesson 74. Read both Bible passages to the children. Talk about how Jesus brought peace to his disciples and how He brings peace to us.

2. Ask the children to draw a picture of their family.

3. Tell them that they will be writing a letter to Jesus asking Him to bring peace the their families.

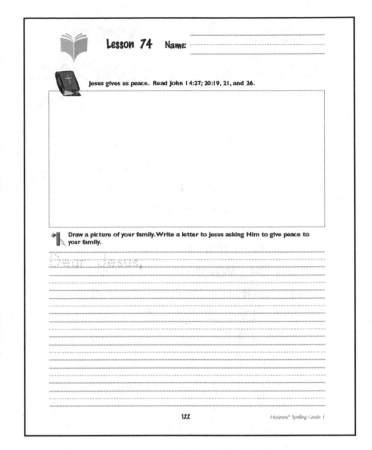

Extended Activity:

Share stories and pictures.

Lesson 75 - Assess and Evaluate Progress

Activities:

1. Give the students Lesson 75. Tell the children that this is a "Check-up" page to see what they have learned during the week. [Note: Teachers/parents of home schoolers may decide what will be assessed. If a child did exceptionally well on the "What do you know?" pre-assessment, the teacher may choose not to test words already known by the child. Or the teacher may choose to test all Words for the Week.]

2. Tell the children that you will say a word. They will listen to the word and to the sentence you will give them. Then, they will write the word on the line next to the numbers. [Lines are given for the weekly words, but make sure to also check the Working Words for the week.]

3. Say the word. Repeat it in the context of a sentence. Repeat the word.

4. The children write the word dictated in the **Test** column.

5. The process is repeated until all words have been tested.

6. The teacher may correct in class by writing the words on the board and having the children compare or "self-correct" their work. Or the teacher may correct each child's work individually.

7. The teacher then uses the **Correction** column to write any corrections for words misspelled.

8. In the **Practice** column, the child copies the correct spelling of any words missed.

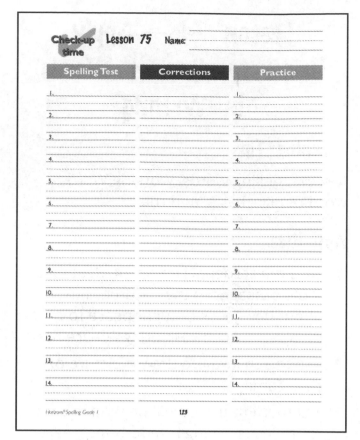

9. The second side of the page can be used for retesting, for testing additional sight or "Working Words" added for the week, and for additional practice.

Extended Activity:

Review any words missed.

Week 16

Lessons 76-80: Assess Child's Knowledge

Goal: To review words from Lessons 41–75.

What Do You Remember?

Give the students the What do you remember? page for Lessons 41-75. Tell them that this page will be used to see what they remember about the words they have studied so far this year. Select an additional four to six Working Words from the list of words added each week. Ask them to listen carefully to each word as you say it, repeat it in a sentence, and say it once again. Follow the procedures for this page as described in the *Introduction* at the beginning of this Teacher's Guide.

NOTE: If you have kept records of words that each child continues to find difficult, you may want to adjust the words in this unit to fit the needs of the individual child. Replace review words already mastered with those still needing work.

What do you remember — Lessons 41–75   Name: _____

Write the words your teacher reads.

1.	13.	25.
your	some	good
2. love	14. most	26. great
3. blue	15. kindest	27. sister
4. you	16. faster	28. brother
5. friend	17. other	
6. can't	18. playful	
7. I'm	19. happiness	
8. you're	20. spelling	
9. very	21. night	
10. people	22. write	
11. classes	23. back	
12. boxes	24. know	

Horizons Spelling Grade 1   115

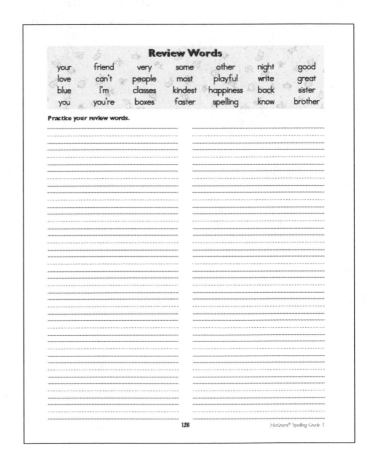

Review Words

your	friend	very	some	other	night	good
love	can't	people	most	playful	write	great
blue	I'm	classes	kindest	happiness	back	sister
you	you're	boxes	faster	spelling	know	brother

Practice your review words.

126   *Horizons® Spelling Grade 1*

Lesson 76 - Introduce Words

Activities:

1. Give the students Lesson 76. (The activities in this lesson can be used for independent review of concepts if the children are able.) Read the directions for the first activity. Ask the children to look carefully at the words in the blue word box. Have them find the three contractions in the box and write them on the lines. Ask them to write out what each contraction stands for on the line next to the contraction.

2. In Activity 2, review the words with the children. Ask them to circle all silent letters in each word. Remind them not to forget to include silent **e**.

3. Read the words in the word box for Activity 3. Ask the children to write them in ABC order. Check.

Extended Activities for the Week:

1. Use the sheets, charts, or booklets created for the word family exercises to help the children review all the words studied to date, not simply those included in the lesson. Include all Working Words given in the weeks prior to this one.

2. Have the children use the review spelling words in sentences.

3. Reproducible *Week 16 Worksheet* for in-class or take-home use.

Lesson 77 - Examine and Explore Words

Teaching Tip:

Review selected Working Words, spelling words, and rules.

Activities:

1. Give the students Lesson 77. Ask the children to read the words in the yellow word box. Read the directions for the first activity. Ask the children to select a review spelling word from the box that rhymes with each word printed in Activity 1. Have the children write the words on the lines provided. Check.

2. Read the second direction. Ask the children to read the definition or word given for each number in Activity 2. Ask them to select a word from the box that will go with the definition. Have them write the word on the line provided. Check.

Extended Activities:

1. Review concepts given in the activities on pp. 127 and 128, as needed, for individual students.

2. Review all word family charts which apply to these lessons.

Lesson 78 - Look at Context and Meaning of Words

Teaching Tip:

Review sentence construction: capitals, periods, questions marks, etc.

Activities:

1. Give the students Lesson 78. Explain to the children that they will be writing their own sentences, using the spelling word or words provided in the word box for each sentence.

2. Unless there is some special difficulty, allow the children to complete this activity independently.

3. Check and share sentences.

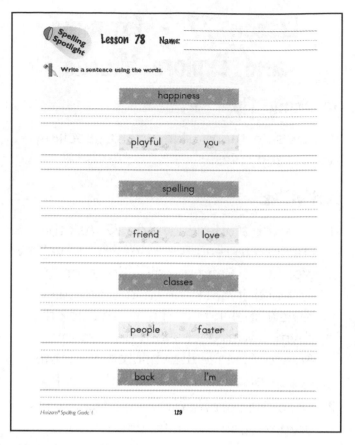

Extended Activities:

1. Review concepts as needed.

2. Review scripture verses used in the last eight weeks.

Lesson 79 - Apply Understanding of Words in Writing

Teaching Tips:

1. Review spelling words, working words, word family charts, and rules.
2. Have *Spelling Dictionary* available.

Activities:

1. Give the students Lesson 79. Review the words in the box with the children.
2. Explain that they will write a their own story, using the words from the box and any other words they choose.
3. Brainstorm ideas on the board as needed.
4. Allow children to write their stories, helping those who have difficulties.

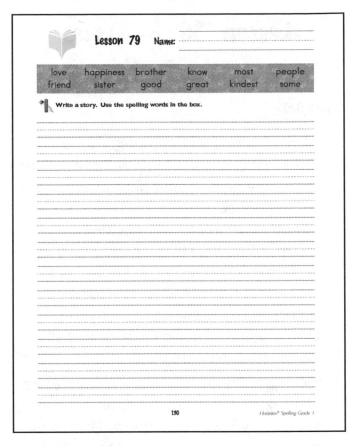

Extended Activities:

1. Share stories.
2. Draw pictures for stories.

Lesson 80 - Assess and Evaluate Progress

Activities:

1. Give the students Lesson 80. Tell the children that this is a "Check-up" page to see what they have remembered from the last eight weeks. [Note: Teachers/parents of home schoolers may decide what will be assessed. If a child did exceptionally well on the "What do you know?" pre-assessment, the teacher may choose not to test words already known by the child. Or the teacher may choose to test all Words for the Week.]

2. Tell the children that you will say a word. They will listen to the word and to the sentence you will give them. Then, they will write the word on the line next to the numbers. [Lines are given for the weekly words, but make sure to also check the Working Words for the week.]

3. Say the word. Repeat it in the context of a sentence. Repeat the word.

4. The children write the word dictated in the **Test** column.

5. The process is repeated until all words have been tested.

6. The teacher may correct in class by writing the words on the board and having the children compare or "self-correct" their work. Or the teacher may correct each child's work individually.

7. The teacher then uses the **Correction** column to write any corrections for words misspelled.

8. In the **Practice** column, the child copies the correct spelling of any words missed.

Check-up time   Lesson 80   Name:

Write the words your teacher reads.

1.   13.   25.
2.   14.   26.
3.   15.   27.
4.   16.   28.
5.   17.
6.   18.
7.   19.
8.   20.
9.   21.
10.   22.
11.   23.
12.   24.

Horizons Spelling Grade 1   191

9. The second side of the page can be used for retesting, for testing additional sight or "Working Words" added for the week, and for additional practice.

Extended Activity:

Review any words missed.

Week 17

Lessons 81-85: Assess Child's Knowledge

Goal: To recognize and spell words with **ou**, **ow**, **au**, and **aw**.

Rule: A vowel diphthong is two vowels that blend together to make one sound. The diphthongs **ow** and **ou** stand for the sounds heard in **auto**, **brown**, and **snow**.

Rule: A vowel diphthong is two vowels that blend together to make one sound. Examples: **ow** and **ou, owl**, **own**, **south**.

Rule: The vowel diphthong **ow** can make two sounds: **ow** as in **cow**, or **ow** as in **snow**.

Rule: Vowel digraphs are two vowels put together in a word that make a long or short sound, or have a special sound all their own. The vowel digraphs **au** and **aw** stand for the sounds heard in **saw** and **auto**.

What Do You Know?

Give the students the What do you know? page for Lessons 81-85. Tell them that this page will be used to see what they already know about the Words for the Week. Ask them to listen carefully to each word as you say it, repeat it in a sentence, and say it once again. Follow the procedures for this page as described in the Introduction at the beginning of this Teacher's Guide.

Ask the children to write their Working Words for the week in the word box and on their own paper.

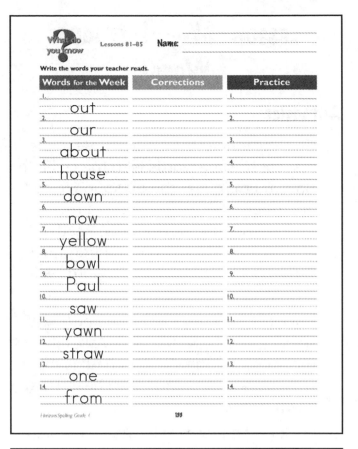

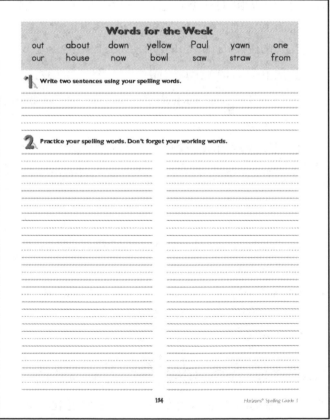

Show the children how to write their Working Words in the appropriate section at the back of their *Spelling Dictionary*.

Lesson 81 - Introduce Words

Activities:

1. Give the students Lesson 81. Read the first six spelling words with the children. Have them repeat the **ou** sound in **out**, **our**, **about**, **house**. Have them repeat the **ow** sound in **down**, **now**. Read the next two words. Ask the children what sound the **ow** makes in the words **yellow**, **bowl** (long **ō**).

2. Have the children look at the **au/aw** spelling words. Read them. Ask them if the **au** sound they hear in **Paul** is the same as the **aw** sound they hear in **saw**, **yawn**, **straw**.

3. Look at the first activity. Ask the children to look at the word shapes, the words, and the pictures. Ask the children to complete the following tasks:

   a. Find the word that fits its shape.

   b. Write the word in the proper shape box.

   c. Draw a line from the shape to the word.

   d. Draw a line from the word to the correct picture.

   e. Repeat the process for the remaining words, or allow children to work individually.

4. In Activity 2, have the children write the four Working Words and draw the shape of each.

Extended Activities for the Week:

1. Reproducible *Week 17 Worksheet* for in-class or take-home use.

   Begin building recognition by working

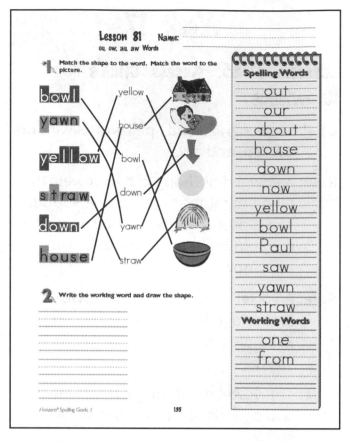

with word families. Make a word family page for the **ou** sound in **out** and the **ow** sound in **now**.

Begin another word family page for the **ow** sound (long **ō**) in **bowl**.

Begin a word family page for the **aw/au** sound in **saw**, **Paul**.

Begin a word family page for number words.

Work with the children, or instruct parents to work with the children, to identify as many words as they can think of for each family.

2. Make a class word family chart for each family listed on the worksheet. Hang where children can see it. Add words as they are learned. Highlight or check off words that are part of spelling lessons or reading lessons.

3. Write sentences with the Working Words chosen for the week.

Lesson 82 - Examine and Explore Words

Teaching Tip:

Review spelling words, Working Words, word family charts, and rules.

Activities:

1. Give the students Lesson 82. Practice some scrambled words on the board with the children before working the page. Have the children refer to the Working Words list from the previous lesson.

2. Write the Words for the Week on the chalkboard or whiteboard and review them with the children. Look at the first house in Activity 1. Ask the children to look at the spelling words on the board and try to unscramble the word in the first house. Make sure that the children write the word **saw** and not the word **was**, which is not a spelling word in this unit.

3. If children have trouble with the scrambled words, provide letter cards or Scrabble tiles that can be moved around to form the words correctly. Complete page together or independently as children are able.

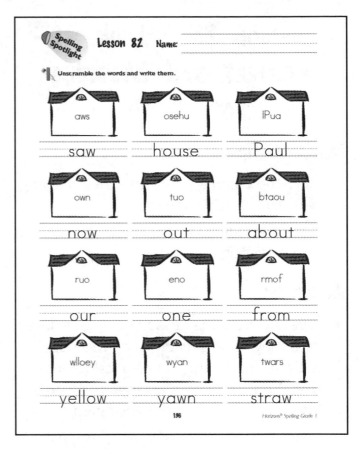

Extended Activities:

1. Add to word family pages and charts.

2. Provide additional practice for children who find the scrambled words difficult. Watch for reversals and any other signs of possible reading disabilities.

Lesson 83 - Look at Context and Meaning of Words

Teaching Tips:

1. Help the children to locate their spelling words in the *Spelling Dictionary*.
2. Review spelling words, Working Words, and rules for the week.

Activities:

1. Give the students Lesson 83. (For children who may have difficulty with this page, provide word cards for each sentence so that the children can arrange the words into a sentence before copying it.)

2. Look at the first word box on the page. Write the words **house**, **yellow**, **My**, **is** on the board. Tell the children that these words can be made into a sentence. Ask them what word has a clue that tells them it will begin the sentence (**My** begins with a capital letter). Help them to make a sentence with the words: **My house is yellow.** Remind them that a sentence ends with a period. Have the children copy the sentence on the line provided. Proceed in the same manner with the remaining sentences unless children are able to work independently.
NOTE: Two lines are provided for two different arrangements of the third sentence. Either answer is acceptable.

3. Read the Bible verses to the children. Discuss the story of Paul's escape with them. Ask them for the details they remember.

Extended Activities:

1. Have the children create their own scrambled sentences. They might work in pairs. When they have finished, ask them to exchange their sentences for their partners to solve.

2. Act out the story of Paul's escape.

Lesson 84 - Apply Understanding of Words in Writing

Teaching Tip:

Review spelling words, Working Words, and the story of Paul's escape.

Activities:

1. Give the students Lesson 84. Review the story of Paul's escape. Tell the children to think of a part of the story they would like to draw. Ask them to draw their pictures.

2. When they have finished their pictures, ask them to write the story as they remember it. Help as needed. Put any words related to the story that are not spelling words on the board. Share stories and check.

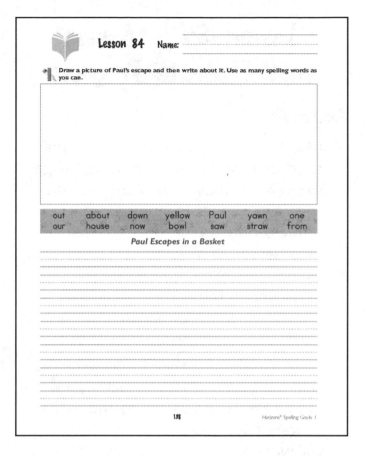

| out | about | down | yellow | Paul | yawn | one |
| our | house | now | bowl | saw | straw | from |

Paul Escapes in a Basket

Lesson 85 - Assess and Evaluate Progress

Activities:

1. Give the students Lesson 85. Tell the children that this is a "Check-up" page to see what they have learned during the week. [Note: Teachers/parents of home schoolers may decide what will be assessed. If a child did exceptionally well on the "What do you know?" pre-assessment, the teacher may choose not to test words already known by the child. Or the teacher may choose to test all Words for the Week.]

2. Tell the children that you will say a word. They will listen to the word and to the sentence you will give them. Then, they will write the word on the line next to the numbers. [Lines are given for the weekly words, but make sure to also check the Working Words for the week.]

3. Say the word. Repeat it in the context of a sentence. Repeat the word.

4. The children write the word dictated in the **Test** column.

5. The process is repeated until all words have been tested.

6. The teacher may correct in class by writing the words on the board and having the children compare or "self-correct" their work. Or the teacher may correct each child's work individually.

7. The teacher then uses the **Correction** column to write any corrections for words misspelled.

8. In the **Practice** column, the child copies the correct spelling of any words missed.

9. The second side of the page can be used for retesting, for testing additional sight or "Working Words" added for the week, and for additional practice.

Extended Activity:

Review any words missed.

Week 18

Lessons 86-90: Assess Child's Knowledge

Goal: To recognize and spell words with **oi**, **oy**, and compound words.

Rule: The diphthongs **oi** and **oy** make the sounds in **coin** and **boy**.

Rule: A compound word is a word made from two or more words joined together to make one word.
Examples: **backyard**, **runway**, **mailbox**.
A compound word is divided between the words that make up the compound word.

What Do You Know?

Give the students the What do you know? page for Lessons 86-90. Tell them that this page will be used to see what they already know about the Words for the Week. Ask them to listen carefully to each word as you say it, repeat it in a sentence, and say it once again. Follow the procedures for this page as described in the *Introduction* at the beginning of this Teacher's Guide.

Ask the children to write their Working Words for the week in the word box and on their own paper.

Show the children how to write their Working Words in the appropriate section at the back of their *Spelling Dictionary*.

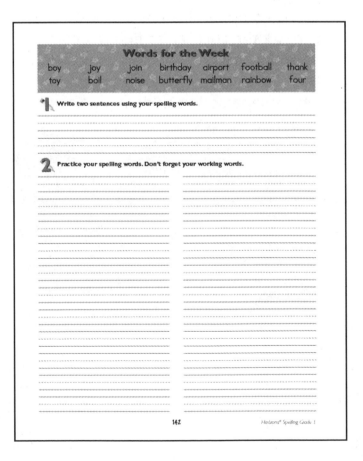

Lesson 86 - Introduce Words

Activities:

1. Give the students Lesson 86. Write **oy** and **oi** on the board. Ask the children to think of words that have the **oy/oi** sound. Write the words they dictate under the appropriate spelling. Look at the first activity on the page. Ask the children to read the spelling words that are spelled with **oy**. Write them on the lines. Ask the children to find the spelling words that are spelled with oi. Write them on the lines.

2. Explain to the children that sometimes we put two words together to make a new word. Demonstrate on the board. Have the children give examples of compound words that they know. Look at the compound words in the spelling list. Ask the children to find the compound words that match the pictures in the box. Help them to write the two words separately and then put them together.

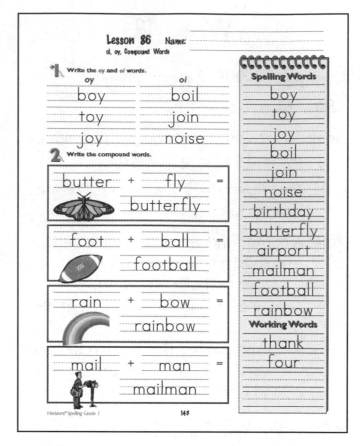

Extended Activities for the Week:

1. Reproducible *Week 18 Worksheet* for in-class or take-home use.

   Begin building recognition by working with word families. Make a word family page for **oi/oy**.

   Begin a word family page for compound words.

   Add to number word page.

   Work with the children, or instruct parents to work with the children, to identify as many words as they can think of for each family.

2. Make a class word family chart for each family listed on the worksheet. Hang where children can see it. Add words as they are learned. Highlight or check off words that are part of spelling lessons or reading lessons.

3. Write sentences with all Working Words chosen for the week.

Lesson 87 - Examine and Explore Words

Teaching Tip:

Review all rules, spelling words, and Working Words for the week.

Activities:

1. Give the students Lesson 87. Tell the children that each set of words in the first activity is a definition for one of the spelling words in the blue word box. Read the first definition. Ask the children to find the spelling word and write it. Ask them to draw a line to the picture of a toy. Repeat the process for the remaining definitions or allow children to work independently.

2. Have the children look at the pictures in Activity 2. Name the pictures. Ask the children to write the spelling word for each picture on the appropriate line.

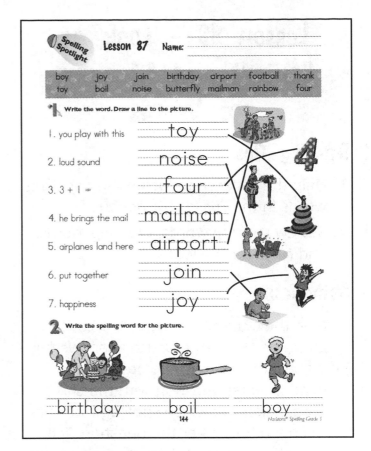

Extended Activities:

1. Add to word family charts and pages.

2. Have children make up definitions for any spelling words not used in the first activity.

Lesson 88 - Look at Context and Meaning of Words

Teaching Tips:

1. Help the children to locate their spelling words in the *Spelling Dictionary*.
2. Review spelling words, Working Words, and rules for the week.

Activities:

1. Give the students Lesson 88. Activity 1 gives the children practice in answering a question with a complete sentence. Read the first question with the children. Ask them which spelling word they will need to answer the question. Tell them that they will write their answer to the question in a complete sentence. Guide them in doing so. Repeat the process for the remaining questions.
2. Read the story of Noah to the children. Talk about the rainbow given as God's promise. Ask the children to color the picture and add to it

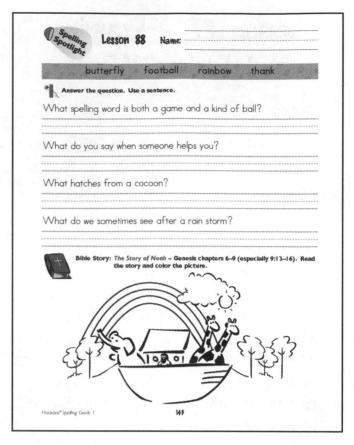

Extended Activities:

1. Have the children act out or make a booklet of the different scenes in the Noah story.
2. Do additional question/answer activities for writing practice.

Lesson 89 - Apply Understanding of Words in Writing

Teaching Tip:

Review spelling words, Working Words, and rules.

Activities:

1. Give the students Lesson 89. Ask the children to talk about times when they have seen a rainbow, or part of a rainbow, in the sky.

2. Have them draw a picture and write about a rainbow they have seen.

Extended Activities:

1. Share stories and pictures with the class.

2. Make corrections as needed on stories.

Lesson 90 - Assess and Evaluate Progress

Activities:

1. Give the students Lesson 90. Tell the children that this is a "Check-up" page to see what they have learned during the week. [Note: Teachers/parents of home schoolers may decide what will be assessed. If a child did exceptionally well on the "What do you know?" pre-assessment, the teacher may choose not to test words already known by the child. Or the teacher may choose to test all Words for the Week.]

2. Tell the children that you will say a word. They will listen to the word and to the sentence you will give them. Then, they will write the word on the line next to the numbers. [Lines are given for the weekly words, but make sure to also check the Working Words for the week.]

3. Say the word. Repeat it in the context of a sentence. Repeat the word.

4. The children write the word dictated in the **Test** column.

5. The process is repeated until all words have been tested.

6. The teacher may correct in class by writing the words on the board and having the children compare or "self-correct" their work. Or the teacher may correct each child's work individually.

7. The teacher then uses the **Correction** column to write any corrections for words misspelled.

8. In the **Practice** column, the child copies the correct spelling of any words missed.

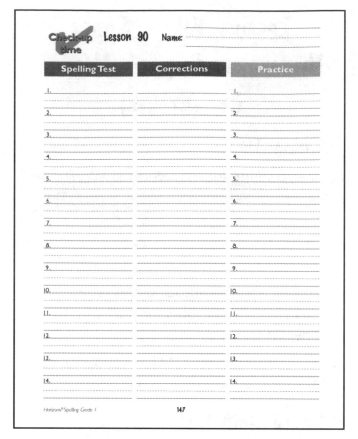

9. The second side of the page can be used for retesting, for testing additional sight or "Working Words" added for the week, and for additional practice.

Extended Activity:

Review any words missed.

Week 19

Lessons 91-95: Assess Child's Knowledge

Goal: To recognize and spell words with **l** and **r** consonant blends.

Rule: In an **r** blend, two or more consonants come together in word. Their sounds blend together, but each sound is heard. Examples: **green**, **frog**, **tree**.

Rule: In an **l** blend, two or more consonants come together in word. Their sounds blend together, but each sound is heard. Examples: **black**, **plant**, **sled**.

What Do You Know?

Give the students the *What do you know?* page for Lessons 91-95. Tell them that this page will be used to see what they already know about the Words for the Week. Ask them to listen carefully to each word as you say it, repeat it in a sentence, and say it once again. Follow the procedures for this page as described in the *Introduction* at the beginning of this Teacher's Guide.

Ask the children to write their Working Words for the week in the word box and on their own paper.

Show the children how to write their Working Words in the appropriate section at the back of their *Spelling Dictionary*.

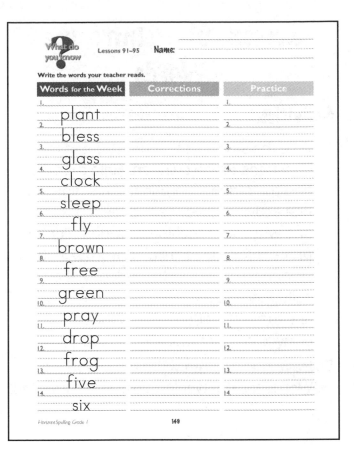

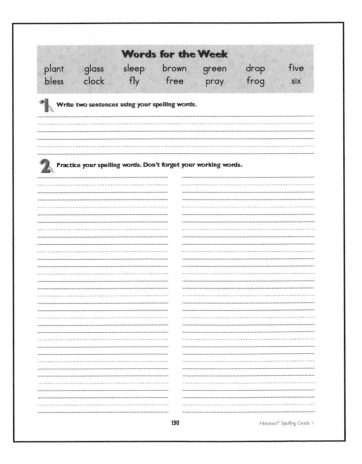

Lesson 91 - Introduce Words

Activities:

1. Give the students Lesson 91. Read the directions to the children. Help them to find the hidden word in the first line of the first activity. Have them circle the word and write it on the line provided. Continue process for the remaining words or allow students to work independently. If any child has visual difficulties with this type of assignment, help them to block out the unnecessary letters.

2. Have the children write their Working Words for the week on the lines provided.

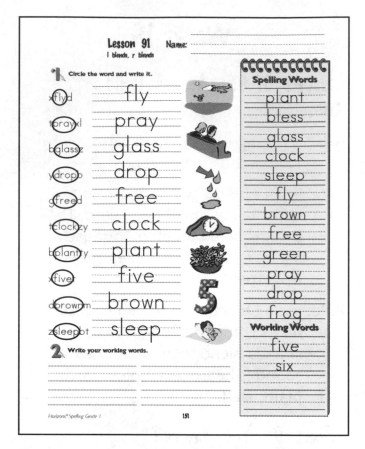

Extended Activities for the Week:

1. Reproducible *Week 19 Worksheet* for in-class or take-home use.

   Begin work family pages for **r** blends and **l** blends.

   Add to page for number words.

   Begin color word page.

2. Make a class word family chart for each family listed on the worksheet. Hang where children can see it. Add words as they are learned. Highlight or check off words that are part of spelling lessons or reading lessons.

3. Write sentences with the Working Words chosen for the week.

Lesson 92 - Examine and Explore Words

Teaching Tip:

Review blends, spelling words, and Working Words.

Activities:

1. Give the students Lesson 92. Ask the children to read the words in the word box. In the first activity, tell the children that they are to find and write the spelling word that rhymes with the word given in the activity. Have children complete activity independently. Check.

2. Ask the children to find two spelling words that are the names of numbers. Tell them to write these two words on the lines provided in Activity 2.

3. Ask the children to find two spelling words that are colors. Write them on the lines provided in Activity 3.

Extended Activities:

1. Continue to add to word family pages and charts.

2. Give added practice for any child who has difficulty with rhyming.

Lesson 93 - Look at Context and Meaning of Words

Teaching Tips:

1. Help the children to locate their spelling words in the *Spelling Dictionary*.

2. Review spelling words, Working Words, and rules for the week.

Activities:

1. Give the students Lesson 93. Review crossword puzzles, especially shared numbers both across and down. Begin with 1 – Across. Ask the children to read the clue, then find the spelling word that fits that clue. Have them note that they are looking for a three-letter word. When they have found and written the word **fly** in the correct boxes, read the clue for 1 – Down. Ask them to find a spelling word beginning with the letter **f** that has four letters and answers the clue given. Have them write the word in **free** in the correct boxes. Proceed in the same manner with the other clues, showing the children how to use letters already written down as additional clues to help them solve the puzzle.

2. Using the spelling word list given on the page, ask the children to solve the word and number puzzles in Activity 2.

3. Read the Bible verse with the children. Have them read it with you. Ask them to find the spelling word in the verse.

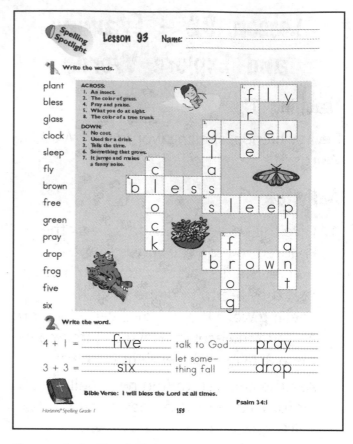

Extended Activities:

1. Have the children, discuss, draw, and/or write ways in which they bless the Lord at all times. Share.

2. Add to word family charts and pages.

Lesson 94 - Apply Understanding of Words in Writing

Teaching Tip:

Review spelling words, Working Words, rules, and rules for sentences.

Activities:

1. Give the students Lesson 94. Tell the children they will be writing a sentence for each set of spelling words given. They will also draw a picture to go with their sentences.

2. Help them with the first one by brain-storming some sentences and possible pictures on the board.

3. Check and share sentences and pictures.

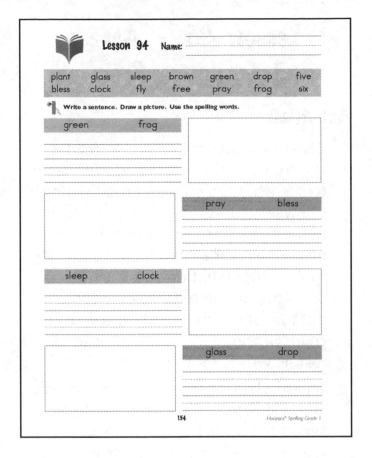

Lesson 95 - Assess and Evaluate Progress

Activities:

1. Give the students Lesson 95. Tell the children that this is a "Check-up" page to see what they have learned during the week. [Note: Teachers/parents of home schoolers may decide what will be assessed. If a child did exceptionally well on the "What do you know?" pre-assessment, the teacher may choose not to test words already known by the child. Or the teacher may choose to test all Words for the Week.]

2. Tell the children that you will say a word. They will listen to the word and to the sentence you will give them. Then, they will write the word on the line next to the numbers. [Lines are given for the weekly words, but make sure to also check the Working Words for the week.]

3. Say the word. Repeat it in the context of a sentence. Repeat the word.

4. The children write the word dictated in the **Test** column.

5. The process is repeated until all words have been tested.

6. The teacher may correct in class by writing the words on the board and having the children compare or "self-correct" their work. Or the teacher may correct each child's work individually.

7. The teacher then uses the **Correction** column to write any corrections for words misspelled.

8. In the **Practice** column, the child copies the correct spelling of any words missed.

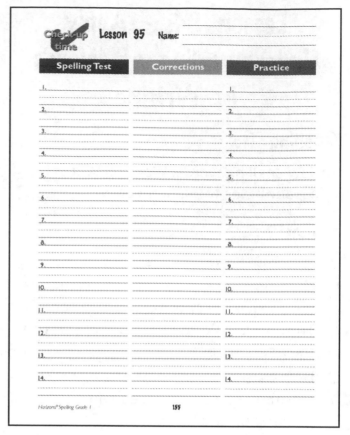

9. The second side of the page can be used for retesting, for testing additional sight or "Working Words" added for the week, and for additional practice.

Extended Activity:

Review any words missed.

Week 20

Lessons 96-100: Assess Child's Knowledge

Goal: To recognize and spell words with beginning **s** blends: **st**, **sl**, **sm**, **sn**, **sk**, and **sp**.

Rule: In an **s** blend, two or more consonants come together in word. Their sounds blend together, but each sound is heard. Examples: **spell**, **snail**.

What Do You Know?

Give the students the What do you know? page for Lessons 96-100. Tell them that this page will be used to see what they already know about the Words for the Week. Ask them to listen carefully to each word as you say it, repeat it in a sentence, and say it once again. Follow the procedures for this page as described in the *Introduction* at the beginning of this Teacher's Guide.

Ask the children to write their Working Words for the week in the word box and on their own paper.

Show the children how to write their Working Words in the appropriate section at the back of their *Spelling Dictionary*.

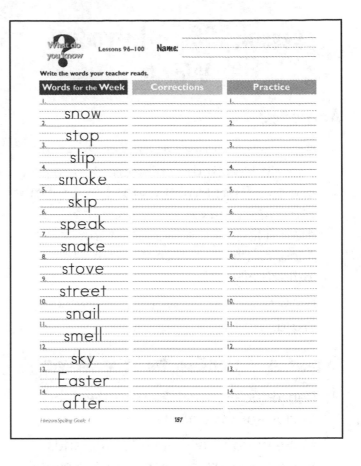

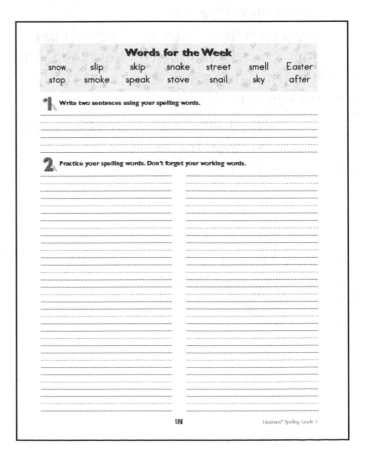

Lesson 96 - Introduce Words

Activities:

1. Give the students Lesson 96. Read the directions with the children. Do the first one together: Find the word that rhymes with **rake** (**snake**); write it on the line; draw a line to the picture of the snake. Allow children to complete this activity individually. Check.

2. Have the children write their Working Words on the lines provided.

Extended Activities for the Week:

1. Reproducible *Week 20 Worksheet* for in-class or take-home use.

   Make word family page for **s** blends. Since there are many **s** blends, several pages may be needed.

   Work with the children, or instruct parents to work with the children, to identify as many words as they can think of for each family.

2. Make a class word family chart for each family listed on the worksheet. Hang where children can see it. Add words as they are learned. Highlight or check off words that are part of spelling lessons or reading lessons.

3. Write sentences with the Working Words chosen for the week.

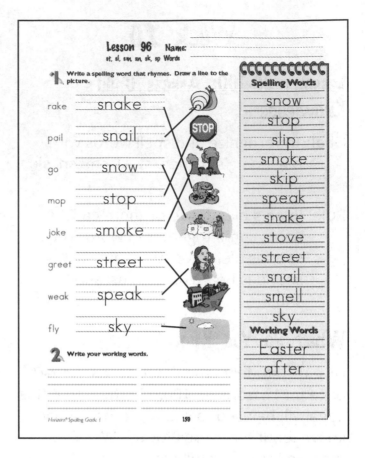

Lesson 97 - Examine and Explore Words

Teaching Tip:

Review spelling words, Working Words, and rules.

Activities:

1. Give the students Lesson 97. Do some preliminary practice on the board. Write the words **stop**, **snow**, **sky**, and **speak** on the board. Help the children to put these words in ABC order using the second letter in the word as their guide.

2. Ask the children to read the words in the purple word box. Ask them to put those words into ABC order. Help as needed or do together as a class.

3. The second activity once again looks at the shapes of words. Letter clues are given as needed. Have the children find the spelling word and write the missing letters in the blue shapes given.

4. Have the children write the two Working Words in the shapes provided. In the space below these words, have the children write and draw the shapes for the two Working Words of choice.

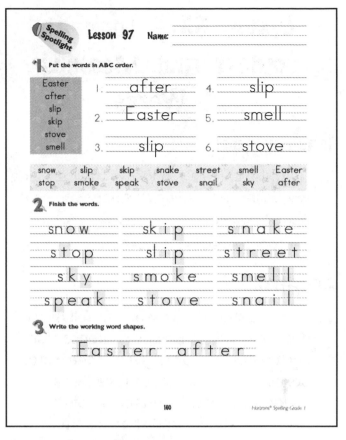

Extended Activities:

1. Add to word family pages.

2. Write sentences with five spelling words of their choice.

3. Give additional practicing in putting words in ABC order using the second letter of words beginning with the same letter.

Lesson 98 - Look at Context and Meaning of Words

Teaching Tips:

1. Help the children to locate their spelling words in the *Spelling Dictionary*.
2. Review spelling words, Working Words, sentence rules, and rules for the week.

Activities:

1. Give the students Lesson 98. Tell the children they will be writing sentences for each group of words given in the word boxes. Do first sentence together as needed. Allow children to complete independently. Check and share sentences.
2. Read the Easter Story to the children from one of the Gospel accounts. Talk about the great wonder of Christ's Resurrection.

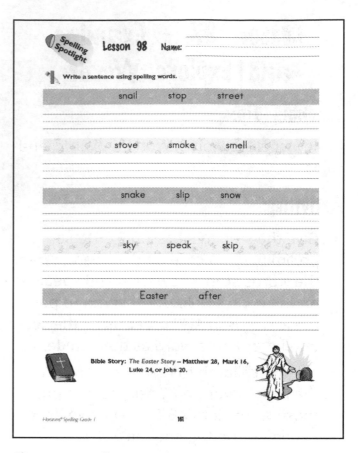

Extended Activities:

1. Read all the Easter accounts and compare them. Have the children tell what things are the same and what are different.
2. Act out one of the Easter accounts.

Lesson 99 - Apply Understanding of Words in Writing

Teaching Tip:

Review spelling words, Working Words, and words related to the Easter story.

Activities:

1. Give the students Lesson 99. Review the Easter story read to the children. Ask them to draw a picture of a part they remember. Ask them to write the story of The First Easter so that they can share it with a friend who does not know about Jesus. Put any additional words needed for this story on the board.

2. Share stories and check.

Extended Activities:

1. Copy stories on good paper to be shared with family and friends as an Easter gift.

2. Make an Easter booklet incorporating all the Easter accounts.

3. Talk about sharing the Easter story with someone who does not know the Good News.

Lesson 100 - Assess and Evaluate Progress

Activities:

1. Give the students Lesson 100. Tell the children that this is a "Check-up" page to see what they have learned during the week. [Note: Teachers/parents of home schoolers may decide what will be assessed. If a child did exceptionally well on the "What do you know?" pre-assessment, the teacher may choose not to test words already known by the child. Or the teacher may choose to test all Words for the Week.]

2. Tell the children that you will say a word. They will listen to the word and to the sentence you will give them. Then, they will write the word on the line next to the numbers. [Lines are given for the weekly words, but make sure to also check the Working Words for the week.]

3. Say the word. Repeat it in the context of a sentence. Repeat the word.

4. The children write the word dictated in the **Test** column.

5. The process is repeated until all words have been tested.

6. The teacher may correct in class by writing the words on the board and having the children compare or "self-correct" their work. Or the teacher may correct each child's work individually.

7. The teacher then uses the **Correction** column to write any corrections for words misspelled.

8. In the **Practice** column, the child copies the correct spelling of any words missed.

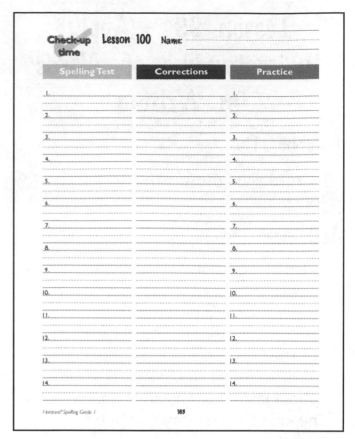

9. The second side of the page can be used for retesting, for testing additional sight or "Working Words" added for the week, and for additional practice.

Extended Activity:

Review any words missed.

Week 21

Lessons 101-105: Assess Child's Knowledge

Goal: To recognize and spell words beginning with **sh** and **th**.

Rule: A consonant digraph is two or more consonants put together that make one sound. Examples: **shoe, show, shirt**.

Rule: A consonant digraph is two or more consonants put together that make one sound. Examples: **the, that, three**.

What Do You Know?

Give the students the What do you know? page for Lessons 101-105. Tell them that this page will be used to see what they already know about the Words for the Week. Ask them to listen carefully to each word as you say it, repeat it in a sentence, and say it once again. Follow the procedures for this page as described in the *Introduction* at the beginning of this Teacher's Guide.

Ask the children to write their Working Words for the week in the word box and on their own paper.

Show the children how to write their Working Words in the appropriate section at the back of their *Spelling Dictionary*.

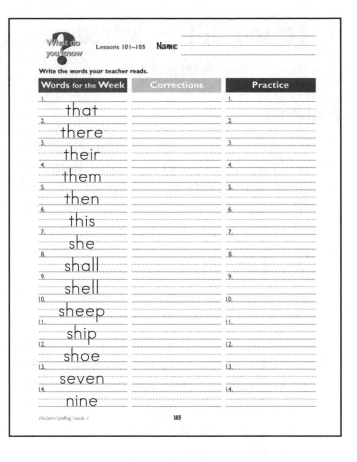

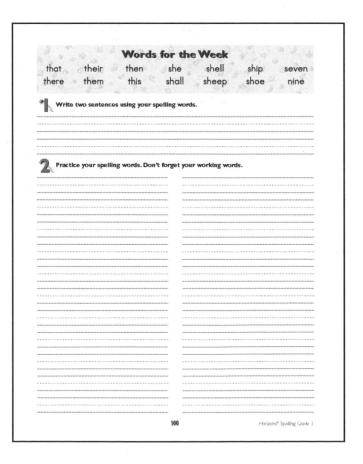

Lesson 101 - Introduce Words

Activities:

1. Give the students Lesson 101. Read the spelling words again with the children. Ask them what two spelling words sound exactly the same, but have different spellings (**there**, **their**). Write these two words on the board. Demonstrate their use in sentences so that the children begin to understand the difference in meaning between the two.

2. In Activity 1, ask the children to copy all of the **th** words onto the lines provided. Tell them to say the word as they write it. Repeat process for the **sh** words.

3. In Activity 2, ask the children to find and write the two spelling words that stand for numbers.

4. Write additional Working Words in the space provided.

Extended Activities for the Week:

1. Reproducible *Week 21 Worksheet* for in-class or take-home use.

   Make word family pages for both **sh** and **th**.

   Add to number family page.

   Begin word family page for pronouns.

   Work with the children, or instruct parents to work with the children, to identify as many words as they can think of for each family.

2. Make a class word family chart for each family listed on the worksheet. Hang where children can see it. Add words as they are learned. Highlight or check off words that are part of spelling lessons or reading lessons.

3. Write sentences with the Working Words chosen for the week.

Lesson 102 - Examine and Explore Words

Teaching Tip:

Review spelling words, Working Words, meanings of **there**/**their**, and rules.

Activities:

1. Give the students Lesson 102. Ask the children to read the clue for each number in Activity 1. Have them find the spelling word that fits the clue and write it on the line provided.

2. In Activity 2, tell the children to look at their spelling words again. Ask them which words can stand for people. Have them find the three words and write them on the line. Some preparation and drill for pronouns may be needed here. Examples: **he**, **him**, **I**, **me**, etc.

3. In Activity 3, ask the children to look at the spelling words and to tell what three words they would use to point to something. Some sentences on the board may be needed to demonstrate this. Examples:
Look at _____ . **Look over** _____ .

Extended Activities:

1. Additional practice may be needed with pronouns that stand for people.

2. Give additional sentence practice for the words there and their.

3. Add to word family charts and pages.

Lesson 103 - Look at Context and Meaning of Words

Teaching Tips:

1. Help the children to locate their spelling words in the *Spelling Dictionary*.

2. Review spelling words, meanings of **there/their**, Working Words, and rules for the week.

Activities:

1. Give the students Lesson 103. Have the children read the first sentence, omitting the choice words. Ask them to look at the word choices for completing the sentence. Ask them to read the sentence again with the words they have chosen. Check. Ask them to circle the word they have chosen for each blank. Check to see that the correct spelling/usage of **there/their** has been selected. Have them write the word in the space provided. Read the completed sentence. Continue this procedure for the remaining sentences in this activity.

2. Read the stories about the Good Shepherd. Discuss them with the children. Have them color the picture adding any details that they wish.

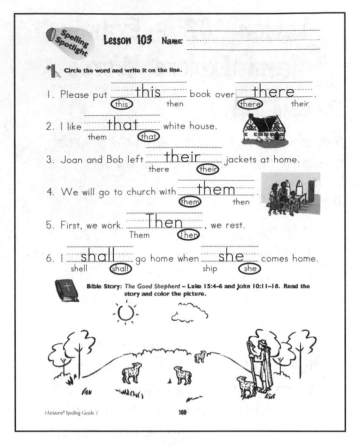

Extended Activities:

1. Give additional sentence practice if needed.

2. Retell or act out the Good Shepherd stories.

Lesson 104 - Apply Understanding of Words in Writing

Teaching Tip:

Review spelling words, meanings of there/their, Working Words, word family charts, and Good Shepherd stories.

Activities:

1. Give the students Lesson 104. Talk about the Good Shepherd stories with the children. Write any words (not given in the yellow word box) they may need on the board.

2. Have the children draw a picture for the Good Shepherd story of their choice.

3. Ask them to write about the Good Shepherd and how he cares for them.

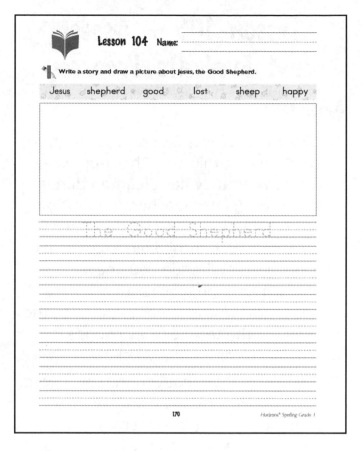

Lesson 105 - Assess and Evaluate Progress

Activities:

1. Give the students Lesson 105. Tell the children that this is a "Check-up" page to see what they have learned during the week. [Note: Teachers/parents of home schoolers may decide what will be assessed. If a child did exceptionally well on the "What do you know?" pre-assessment, the teacher may choose not to test words already known by the child. Or the teacher may choose to test all Words for the Week.]

2. Tell the children that you will say a word. They will listen to the word and to the sentence you will give them. Then, they will write the word on the line next to the numbers. [Lines are given for the weekly words, but make sure to also check the Working Words for the week.]

3. Say the word. Repeat it in the context of a sentence. Repeat the word.

4. The children write the word dictated in the **Test** column.

5. The process is repeated until all words have been tested.

6. The teacher may correct in class by writing the words on the board and having the children compare or "self-correct" their work. Or the teacher may correct each child's work individually.

7. The teacher then uses the **Correction** column to write any corrections for words misspelled.

8. In the **Practice** column, the child copies the correct spelling of any words missed.

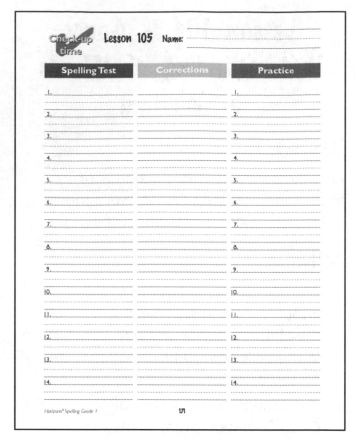

9. The second side of the page can be used for retesting, for testing additional sight or "Working Words" added for the week, and for additional practice.

Extended Activity:

Review any words missed.

Week 22

Lessons 106-110: Assess Child's Knowledge

Goal: To recognize and spell words with the **ch** and **ck** wounds.

Rule: A consonant digraph is two or more consonants put together that make one sound. Examples: **chair**, **chin**, **chip**.

Rule: Consonant digraph **ch** makes the sound as in the beginning of **chair**. Examples: **chair**, **choose**. It can also make the **k** sound. Example: **chorus**.

What Do You Know?

Give the students the What do you know? page for Lessons 106-110. Tell them that this page will be used to see what they already know about the Words for the Week. Ask them to listen carefully to each word as you say it, repeat it in a sentence, and say it once again. Follow the procedures for this page as described in the *Introduction* at the beginning of this Teacher's Guide.

Ask the children to write their Working Words for the week in the word box and on their own paper.

Show the children how to write their Working Words in the appropriate section at the back of their *Spelling Dictionary*.

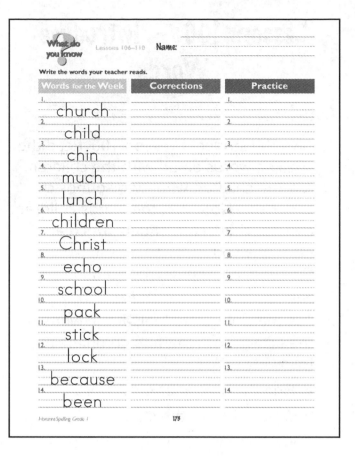

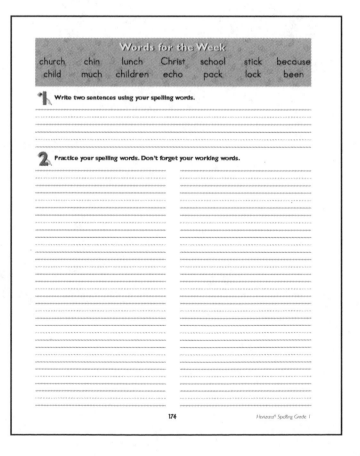

Lesson 106 - Introduce Words

Activities:

1. Give the students Lesson 106. Read the spelling words aloud with the children. Ask the children what two sounds **ch** can make. Note that the words **children**, **church**, **child**, **chin**, **much**, **lunch** all have one sound for **ch**. In the words **Christ**, **echo**, **school**, the **ch** makes a **k** sound.

2. Ask the children to look at the word in the activity. Ask them to complete the following tasks:

   a. Find the shape for each word.

   b. Draw a line to the shape.

   c. Write the word in the shape boxes.

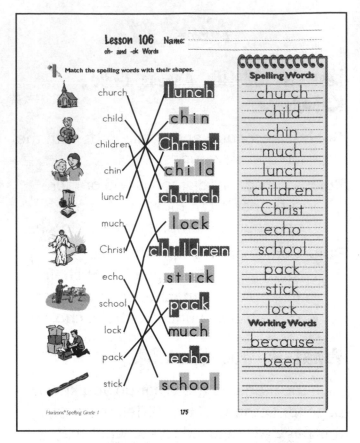

Extended Activities for the Week:

1. Reproducible *Week 22 Worksheet* for in-class or take-home use.

   Make word family pages for **ch** (both hard and soft sounds) and **ck**.

2. Make a class word family chart for each family listed on the worksheet. Hang where children can see it. Add words as they are learned. Highlight or check off words that are part of spelling lessons or reading lessons.

3. Write sentences with the Working Words chosen for the week.

Lesson 107 - Examine and Explore Words

Teaching Tip:

Review spelling words, Working Words, and rules.

Activity:

Give the students Lesson 107. Review the different sounds of **ch** and **ck**. Look at the first word box. Ask the children to find the words in which the **ch** makes a **k** sound. Ask them to write the words in the first box filling in the missing letters. Continue with the remaining boxes.

Extended Activities:

1. Add to word family pages.
2. Write sentences for all spelling words.

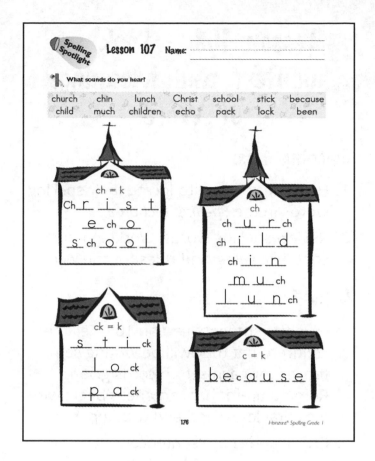

Lesson 108 - Look at Context and Meaning of Words

Teaching Tips:

1. Help the children to locate their spelling words in the *Spelling Dictionary*.
2. Review spelling words, Working Words, sentence rules, and rules for the week.

Activities:

1. Give the students Lesson 108. Tell the children that they will be writing sentences for each set of words given. Remind them that sentences begin with a capital letter and end with a period.
2. Check and share sentences.
3. Read the section in Luke's gospel where he speaks of Jesus and the little children. Read the Bible verse to the children. Talk about how Jesus helps little children.

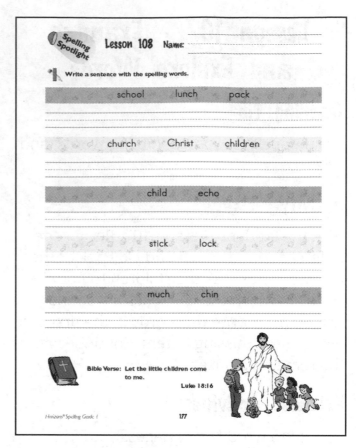

Extended Activities:

1. Have the children memorize and copy the Bible verse.
2. Give additional sentence practice as needed.

Lesson 109 - Apply Understanding of Words in Writing

Teaching Tip:

Review spelling words, Working Words, rules, and Bible verse.

Activities:

1. Give the students Lesson 109. Read and discuss other Bible stories in which Christ showed his love for children by healing them. Have the children share ways in which Christ helps them and their families.

2. Ask the children to color the picture. Have them add themselves to the picture.

3. Ask the children to write a sentence or two about how Christ loves and helps them.

Extended Activities:

1. Share pictures and stories. Add any words misspelled to the list of spelling words for study in the back of the *Spelling Dictionary*.

2. Have the children find ways to share their love for Christ with others.

Lesson 110 - Assess and Evaluate Progress

Activities:

1. Give the students Lesson 110. Tell the children that this is a "Check-up" page to see what they have learned during the week. [Note: Teachers/parents of home schoolers may decide what will be assessed. If a child did exceptionally well on the "What do you know?" pre-assessment, the teacher may choose not to test words already known by the child. Or the teacher may choose to test all Words for the Week.]

2. Tell the children that you will say a word. They will listen to the word and to the sentence you will give them. Then, they will write the word on the line next to the numbers. [Lines are given for the weekly words, but make sure to also check the Working Words for the week.]

3. Say the word. Repeat it in the context of a sentence. Repeat the word.

4. The children write the word dictated in the **Test** column.

5. The process is repeated until all words have been tested.

6. The teacher may correct in class by writing the words on the board and having the children compare or "self-correct" their work. Or the teacher may correct each child's work individually.

7. The teacher then uses the **Correction** column to write any corrections for words misspelled.

8. In the **Practice** column, the child copies the correct spelling of any words missed.

9. The second side of the page can be used for retesting, for testing additional sight or "Working Words" added for the week, and for additional practice.

Extended Activity:

Review any words missed.

Week 23

Lessons 111-115: Assess Child's Knowledge

Goal: To recognize and spell words beginning with **wh** and words ending in **tch**.

Rule: A consonant digraph is two or more consonants put together that make one sound. Examples: **kitchen**, **watch**, **stitch**.

What Do You Know?

Give the students the What do you know? page for Lessons 111-115. Tell them that this page will be used to see what they already know about the Words for the Week. Ask them to listen carefully to each word as you say it, repeat it in a sentence, and say it once again. Follow the procedures for this page as described in the Introduction at the beginning of this Teacher's Guide.

Ask the children to write their Working Words for the week in the word box and on their own paper.

Show the children how to write their Working Words in the appropriate section at the back of their *Spelling Dictionary*.

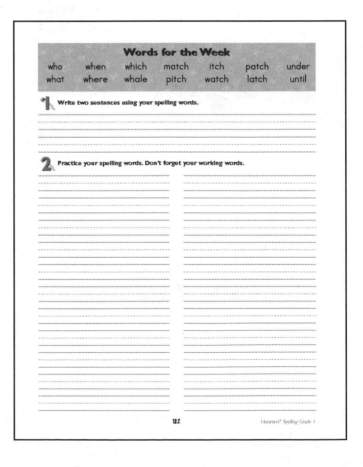

Lesson 111 - Introduce Words

Activities:

1. Give the students Lesson 111. Have the children find the three spelling words that rhyme with match and write them on the lines provided.

2. Write **who**, **what**, **when**, **where**, **which** on the board. Ask the children to use there words in a sentence. Create sentences that use these words as question words. Have the children write the words on the lines provided in Activity 2.

3. Ask the children to find and write the words that go with the two pictures.

4. Have the children write their Working Words.

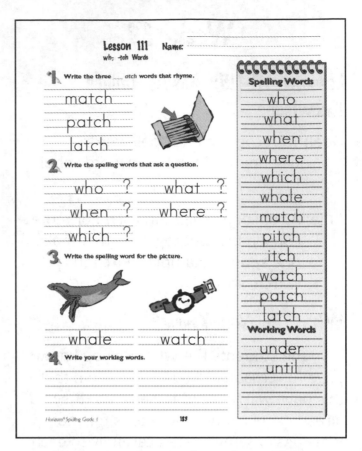

Extended Activities for the Week:

1. Reproducible *Week 23 Worksheet* for in-class or take-home use.

   Make word family pages for **wh** and **tch**.

   Begin a word family page for "position" words: **under**, **over**, **up**, **down**, etc.

   Work with the children, or instruct parents to work with the children, to identify as many words as they can think of for each family

2. Make a class word family chart for each family listed on the worksheet. Hang where children can see it. Add words as they are learned. Highlight or check off words that are part of spelling lessons or reading lessons.

3. Write sentences with the Working Words chosen for the week.

Lesson 112 - Examine and Explore Words

Teaching Tip:

Review spelling words, Working Words, and rules.

Activities:

1. Give the students Lesson 112. Ask the children to study the puzzle and to look for their spelling words hidden in the rows of letters. When they find a spelling word going either across or down a row, they will circle the entire word and then write it on the lines below the puzzle.

2. For children with visual difficulties, provide a card or sheet of paper they can use to isolate each row and make recognition easier.

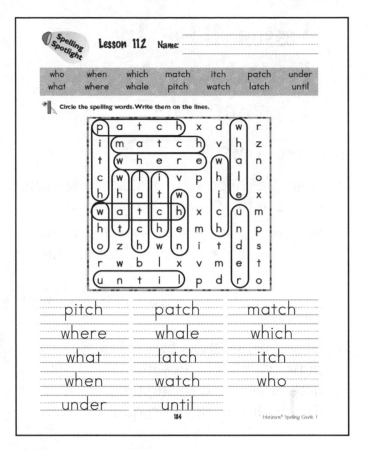

Extended Activities:

1. Write sentences for all spelling words.
2. Add to word family pages.

Lesson 113 - Look at Context and Meaning of Words

Teaching Tips:

1. Help the children to locate their spelling words in the *Spelling Dictionary*.

2. Review spelling words, Working Words, rules for sentences, and rules for the week.

Activities:

1. Give the students Lesson 113. Review punctuation for questions. Read the first sentence in the first activity with the children. Ask which question word will complete the sentence correctly. Have the children write the word in the space provided. Make sure that they use a capital letter. Repeat process for remaining sentences or allow children to complete individually.

2. Read the Bible verse with the children. Talk about the verse and what it might mean to them. Have them write the verse on the lines and then answer the question, Who do they say Jesus is.

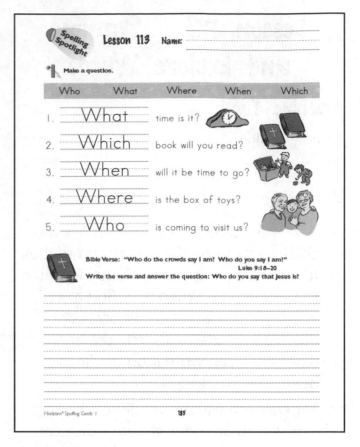

Extended Activities:

1. Provide additional sentence practice as needed.

2. Share responses to Bible verse.

Lesson 114 - Apply Understanding of Words in Writing

Teaching Tip:

Review spelling words, Working Words, and rules.

Activities:

1. Give the students Lesson 114. Tell the children that today they will be completing some rhymes using the spelling words in the word box.

   Have them look at the first picture. Read the first line of the rhyme. What spelling word will complete that line?

2. Read the second line. What spelling word completes the line and rhymes with the word at the end of the first rhyme? Complete remaining rhymes in the same manner.

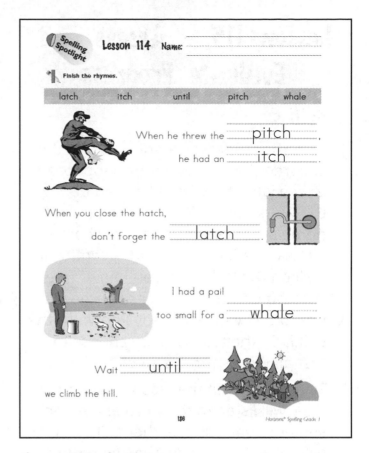

Extended Activity:

Have children create more rhyming couplets using other spelling words.

Lesson 115 - Assess and Evaluate Progress

Activities:

1. Give the students Lesson 115. Tell the children that this is a "Check-up" page to see what they have learned during the week. [Note: Teachers/parents of home schoolers may decide what will be assessed. If a child did exceptionally well on the "What do you know?" pre-assessment, the teacher may choose not to test words already known by the child. Or the teacher may choose to test all Words for the Week.]

2. Tell the children that you will say a word. They will listen to the word and to the sentence you will give them. Then, they will write the word on the line next to the numbers. [Lines are given for the weekly words, but make sure to also check the Working Words for the week.]

3. Say the word. Repeat it in the context of a sentence. Repeat the word.

4. The children write the word dictated in the **Test** column.

5. The process is repeated until all words have been tested.

6. The teacher may correct in class by writing the words on the board and having the children compare or "self-correct" their work. Or the teacher may correct each child's work individually.

7. The teacher then uses the **Correction** column to write any corrections for words misspelled.

8. In the **Practice** column, the child copies the correct spelling of any words missed.

9. The second side of the page can be used for retesting, for testing additional sight or "Working Words" added for the week, and for additional practice.

Extended Activity:

Review any words missed.

Week 24

Lessons 116-120: Assess Child's Knowledge

Goal: To review spelling words from Lessons 81–115.

What Do You Remember?

Give the students the What do you remember? page for Lessons 81-115. Tell them that this page will be used to see what they remember about the words they have studied so far this year. Select an additional four to six Working Words from the list of words added each week. Ask them to listen carefully to each word as you say it, repeat it in a sentence, and say it once again. Follow the procedures for this page as described in the *Introduction* at the beginning of this Teacher's Guide.

NOTE: If you have kept records of words that each child continues to find difficult, you may want to adjust the words in this unit to fit the needs of the individual child. Replace review words already mastered with those still needing work.

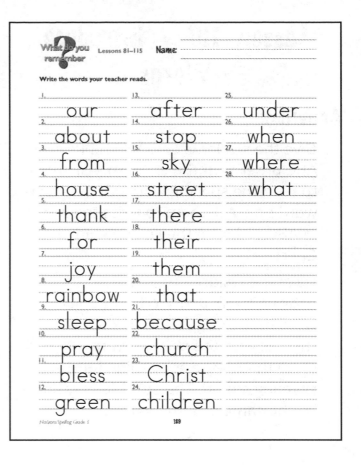

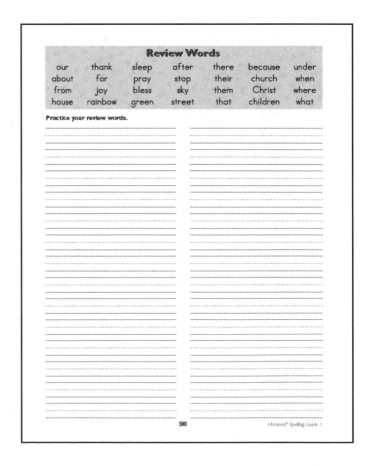

Lesson 116 - Introduce Words

Activities:

1. Give the students Lesson 116. Review ABC order with the children. Ask them to read the spelling words in the green word box. Ask them to write the words in ABC order on the lines provided. Check.

2. Have the children read the words in Activity 2. Ask them to find a spelling word in the large word box above that rhymes with the printed word. Remind them that they are listening for the rhyming sound. The spelling may not be the same as in **flower/our**.

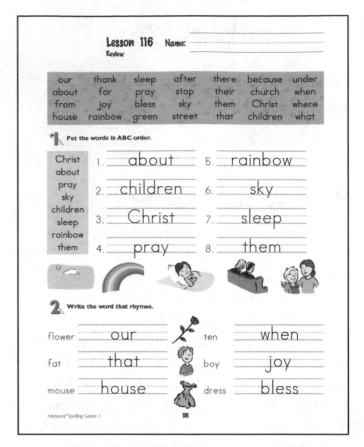

Extended Activities for the Week:

1. Use the sheets, charts, or booklets created for the word family exercises to help the children review all the words studied to date, not simply those included in the lesson. Include all Working Words given in the weeks prior to this one.

2. Have the children use the review Working Words in sentences.

3. Reproducible *Week 24 Worksheet* for in-class or take-home use.

Lesson 117 - Examine and Explore Words

Teaching Tip:

Review spelling words and sentence rules.

Activities:

1. Give the students Lesson 117. In Activity 1, ask the children to look at each picture, to look at the scrambled word below each picture, to find a spelling word for each picture, and to write the word on the line under each picture.

2. In Activity 2, tell the children they are to read the sentence, to decide which word or words will complete the sentence correctly, and to circle the words needed to complete the sentence. Some review of **there/their** may be needed here.

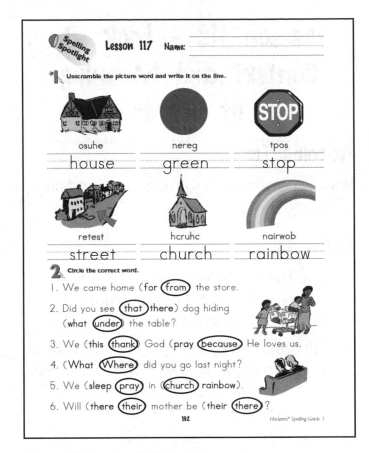

Extended Activities:

1. Provide additional practice with **there/their** if needed.

2. Choose 10 review spelling words and use them in sentences.

Lesson 118 - Look at Context and Meaning of Words

Teaching Tip:

Review punctuation for questions and all sentence rules.

Activities:

1. Give the students Lesson 118. Have the children read the three question words to be used in Activity 1.

2. Tell the children that they will think of a question beginning with each word. Ask them to write their questions. Remind them to end with a question mark.

3. In Activity 2, discuss the two Bible stories represented by the pictures. Ask children to write a sentence about each. Check and share.

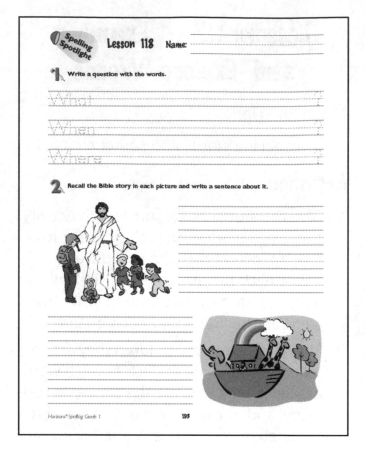

Extended Activities:

1. Give additional practice for any problems with writing questions or sentences.

2. Review appropriate word family charts and pages for this lesson.

Lesson 119 - Apply Understanding of Words in Writing

Activities:

1. Give the students Lesson 119. This is the first time in the spelling lessons that the children are being asked to create a story from "scratch." Review the spelling words in the box. Tell the children that they will stop for a minute and think about the spelling words in the box. What ideas do they get from these words? What pictures do they see? Ask them to write their own stories, using the words in the box and any other words that they need.

2. When their stories are completed, ask them to draw a picture to go with the story. Help as needed. Check and add any misspelled words to the list in the back of the individual *Spelling Dictionary* for further study.

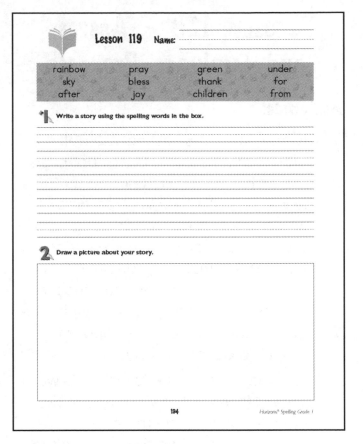

Extended Activities:

1. Share stories and pictures with the class.
2. Review any concepts in this unit that are still weak.

Lesson 120 - Assess and Evaluate Progress

Activities:

1. Give the students Lesson 120. Tell the children that this is a "Check-up" page to see what they have learned during the week. [Note: Teachers/parents of home schoolers may decide what will be assessed. If a child did exceptionally well on the "What do you know?" pre-assessment, the teacher may choose not to test words already known by the child. Or the teacher may choose to test all Words for the Week.]

2. Tell the children that you will say a word. They will listen to the word and to the sentence you will give them. Then, they will write the word on the line next to the numbers. [Lines are given for the weekly words, but make sure to also check the Working Words for the week.]

3. Say the word. Repeat it in the context of a sentence. Repeat the word.

4. The children write the word dictated in the **Test** column.

5. The process is repeated until all words have been tested.

6. The teacher may correct in class by writing the words on the board and having the children compare or "self-correct" their work. Or the teacher may correct each child's work individually.

7. The teacher then uses the **Correction** column to write any corrections for words misspelled.

8. In the **Practice** column, the child copies the correct spelling of any words missed.

Check-up time Lesson 120 Name: _____

Write the words your teacher reads.

1.	13.	25.
2.	14.	26.
3.	15.	27.
4.	16.	28.
5.	17.	
6.	18.	
7.	19.	
8.	20.	
9.	21.	
10.	22.	
11.	23.	
12.	24.	

Horizons Spelling Grade 1   195

9. The second side of the page can be used for retesting, for testing additional sight or "Working Words" added for the week, and for additional practice.

Extended Activity:

Review any words missed.

Week 25

Lessons 121-125: Assess Child's Knowledge

Goal: To recognize and spell words that are synonyms.

Rule: Synonyms are words that have the same or almost the same meaning.

What Do You Know?

Give the students the What do you know? page for Lessons 121-125. Tell them that this page will be used to see what they already know about the Words for the Week. Ask them to listen carefully to each word as you say it, repeat it in a sentence, and say it once again. Follow the procedures for this page as described in the *Introduction* at the beginning of this Teacher's Guide.

Ask the children to write their Working Words for the week in the word box and on their own paper.

Show the children how to write their Working Words in the appropriate section at the back of their *Spelling Dictionary*.

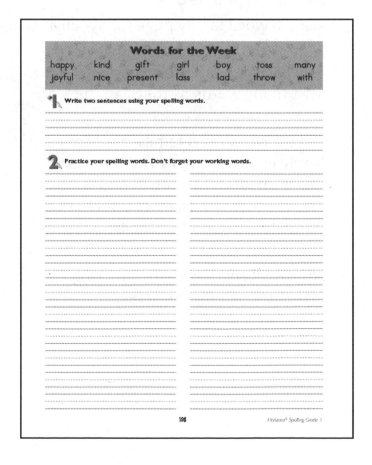

Lesson 121 - Introduce Words

Activities:

1. Give the students Lesson 121. Go over the definition of a synonym with the children. Ask the children to give additional examples of words that have similar meanings. Write them on the board. Review the spelling words. Ask the children to find the spelling words in the puzzle. Give help to children with visual difficulties.

2. Ask the children to write the spelling words they have found on the lines below the puzzle. Check.

Extended Activities for the Week:

1. Reproducible *Week 25 Worksheet* for in-class or take-home use.

   Make a word family page for synonyms.

   Work with the children, or instruct parents to work with the children, to identify as many words as they can think of for each family.

2. Make a class word family chart for each family listed on the worksheet. Hang where children can see it. Add words as they are learned. Highlight or check off words that are part of spelling lessons or reading lessons.

3. Write sentences with the Working Words chosen for the week.

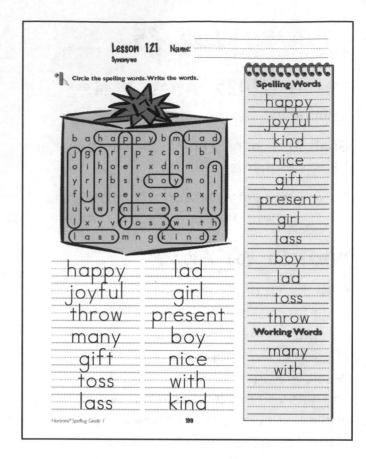

168

Lesson 122 - Examine and Explore Words

Teaching Tip:

Review spelling words and Working Words.

Activities:

1. Give the students Lesson 122. Ask the children to read the directions for the first activity. Have them choose the spelling words what are words for people. Write the words on the lines provided.

2. Have the children read the direction for Activity 2 and complete it. Continue on with the remaining 5 activities on the page.

Extended Activities:

1. Write sentences using 10 spelling words.
2. Add to synonym word family page.

Lesson 123 - Look at Context and Meaning of Words

Teaching Tips:

1. Help the children to locate their spelling words in the *Spelling Dictionary*.
2. Review spelling words, Working Words, and rules for sentences.

Activities:

1. Give the students Lesson 123. Read the first group of spelling words. Ask the children to write a sentence using all three words. Have them draw a picture in the box next to the sentence. Repeat process for the remaining two sentences.

2. Have the children read the Bible verse. Talk about what it means to be kind and patient with those we love. Write the verse on the first line. Ask them to write about something kind they can do on the second line.

Extended Activities:

1. Share Bible verses and ideas.
2. Give added practice in synonyms for those having difficulty.

Lesson 124 - Apply Understanding of Words in Writing

Teaching Tip:

Review spelling words and have *Spelling Dictionary* available for use.

Activities:

1. Give the students Lesson 124. Tell the children that on this page they will be finishing an idea in each sentence. Read the first "sentence starter." Ask the children to think about times when they are happy. Tell them to complete the sentence and to add another sentence if they need to complete what they want to say. Repeat this process for the remaining sentences.

2. Check sentences. Show children how to write the spelling of words they have missed. Add these words to their *Spelling Dictionary* if they are words not already in the dictionary.

Lesson 124   Name: _____

Finish the sentences.

I am happy when _____

The little lad _____

The surprise gift was _____

The children were joyful because _____

The boy will throw _____

202   *Horizons® Spelling Grade 1*

Extended Activities:

1. Check and review sentence construction, punctuation, etc. as needed.

2. Begin putting all word family pages together into booklet form for the children.

Lesson 125 - Assess and Evaluate Progress

Activities:

1. Give the students Lesson 125. Tell the children that this is a "Check-up" page to see what they have learned during the week. [Note: Teachers/parents of home schoolers may decide what will be assessed. If a child did exceptionally well on the "What do you know?" pre-assessment, the teacher may choose not to test words already known by the child. Or the teacher may choose to test all Words for the Week.]

2. Tell the children that you will say a word. They will listen to the word and to the sentence you will give them. Then, they will write the word on the line next to the numbers. [Lines are given for the weekly words, but make sure to also check the Working Words for the week.]

3. Say the word. Repeat it in the context of a sentence. Repeat the word.

4. The children write the word dictated in the **Test** column.

5. The process is repeated until all words have been tested.

6. The teacher may correct in class by writing the words on the board and having the children compare or "self-correct" their work. Or the teacher may correct each child's work individually.

7. The teacher then uses the **Correction** column to write any corrections for words misspelled.

8. In the **Practice** column, the child copies the correct spelling of any words missed.

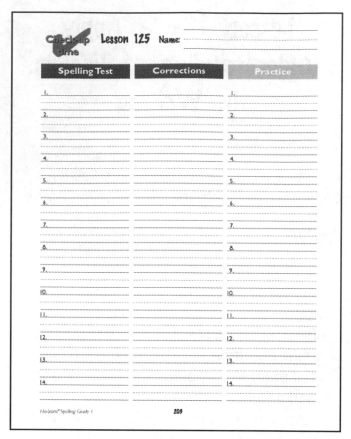

9. The second side of the page can be used for retesting, for testing additional sight or "Working Words" added for the week, and for additional practice.

Extended Activity:

Review any words missed.

Week 26

Lessons 126-130: Assess Child's Knowledge

Goal: To recognize and spell words that are antonyms.

Rule: Antonyms are words that are opposite or almost opposite in meaning.

What Do You Know?

Give the students the What do you know? page for Lessons 126-130. Tell them that this page will be used to see what they already know about the Words for the Week. Ask them to listen carefully to each word as you say it, repeat it in a sentence, and say it once again. Follow the procedures for this page as described in the *Introduction* at the beginning of this Teacher's Guide.

Ask the children to write their Working Words for the week in the word box and on their own paper.

Show the children how to write their Working Words in the appropriate section at the back of their *Spelling Dictionary*.

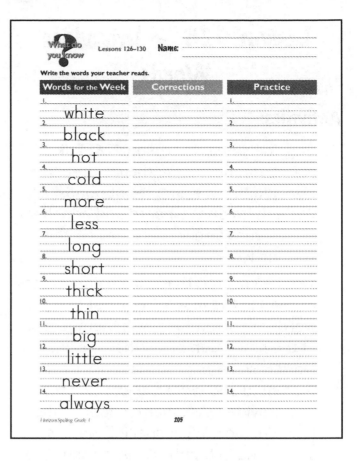

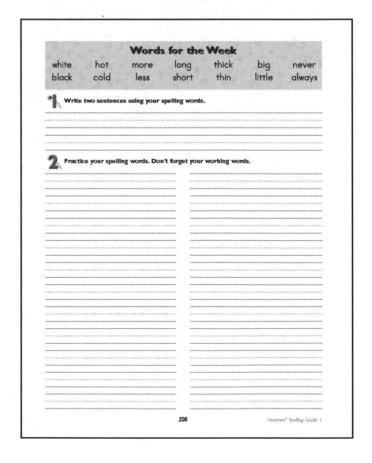

Lesson 126 - Introduce Words

Activities:

1. Give the students Lesson 126. Talk about antonyms. Ask the children to give additional examples of opposites. Write them on the board and add them to the word family chart. Review the spelling words.

2. Tell the children that each pair of words is given in the first activity, but the words are scrambled. Ask them to look at the first green box. What spelling word is scrambled in that box? Have them find and write the word on the line provided. Ask them to look at the first blue box. What spelling word is scrambled in that box? Have them find and write the word on the line provided. Is it the opposite of the first word? Repeat the process for the remaining pairs of words.

Extended Activities for the Week:

1. Reproducible *Week 26 Worksheet* for in-class or take-home use.

   Make a word family page for antonyms. Work with the children, or instruct parents to work with the children, to identify as many words as they can think of for each family.

2. Make a class word family chart for each family listed on the worksheet. Hang where children can see it. Add words as they are learned. Highlight or check off words that are part of spelling lessons or reading lessons.

3. Write sentences with the Working Words chosen for the week.

Lesson 127 - Examine and Explore Words

Teaching Tip:

Review antonyms and all spelling and Working Words.

Activity:

Give the students Lesson 127.
Review the spelling words in the word box.
Ask the children to find the spelling word needed to complete each of the sentences in this activity.

Extended Activities:

1. Create sentence for spelling words not used in this activity: **black**, **short**, **more**, **less**, **never**, **always**.

2. Add to antonym word family page.

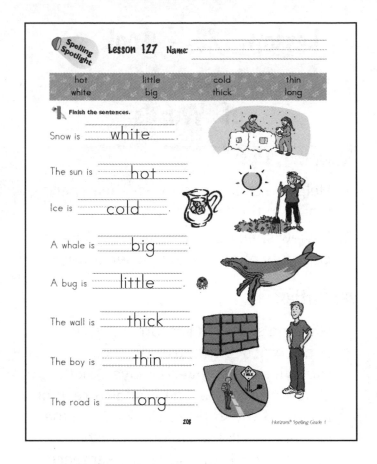

Lesson 128 - Look at Context and Meaning of Words

Teaching Tips:

1. Help the children to locate their spelling words in the *Spelling Dictionary*.

2. Review spelling words, Working Words, concepts of **more/less**; **never/always**.

Activities:

1. Give the students Lesson 128. Give some practice with the ideas of **more/less** and **never/always**. Ask the children to look at the first picture. John and Judy are stacking blocks. Read the sentence. Ask the children which spelling word completes the sentence accurately. Have them circle the word and write it in the space provided. Repeat this process for the remaining sentences.

2. Read the story of David and Goliath to the children. Have the children color the picture and add any details from the story that they like.

Extended Activities:

1. On separate paper, have the children tell the story of David and Goliath.

   OR

2. Have the children put together a play about the story of David and Goliath.

Lesson 129 - Apply Understanding of Words in Writing

Teaching Tip:

Review opposites and sentence rules.

Activities:

1. Give the students Lesson 129. Read and discuss the word pairs at the top of the page. Tell the children that they will pick two pairs of words and create a story using them. Brainstorm some ideas as needed.

2. After the children write their stories, ask them to illustrate the story.

Extended Activities:

1. Share stories.
2. Add any misspelled words to child's list.

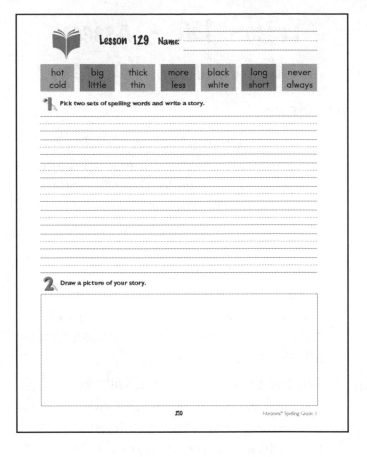

Lesson 130 - Assess and Evaluate Progress

Activities:

1. Give the students Lesson 130. Tell the children that this is a "Check-up" page to see what they have learned during the week. [Note: Teachers/parents of home schoolers may decide what will be assessed. If a child did exceptionally well on the "What do you know?" pre-assessment, the teacher may choose not to test words already known by the child. Or the teacher may choose to test all Words for the Week.]

2. Tell the children that you will say a word. They will listen to the word and to the sentence you will give them. Then, they will write the word on the line next to the numbers. [Lines are given for the weekly words, but make sure to also check the Working Words for the week.]

3. Say the word. Repeat it in the context of a sentence. Repeat the word.

4. The children write the word dictated in the **Test** column.

5. The process is repeated until all words have been tested.

6. The teacher may correct in class by writing the words on the board and having the children compare or "self-correct" their work. Or the teacher may correct each child's work individually.

7. The teacher then uses the **Correction** column to write any corrections for words misspelled.

8. In the **Practice** column, the child copies the correct spelling of any words missed.

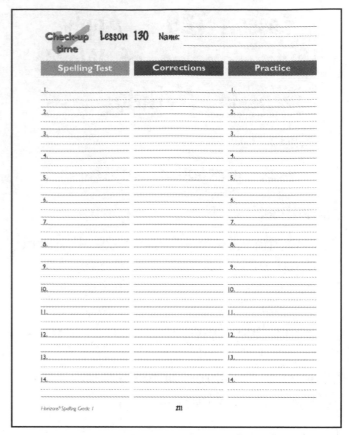

9. The second side of the page can be used for retesting, for testing additional sight or "Working Words" added for the week, and for additional practice.

Extended Activity:

Review any words missed.

Week 27

Lessons 131-135: Assess Child's Knowledge

Goal: To recognize and spell words that are homophones.

Rule: Homophones are words that sound alike but have different spellings and different meanings.

What Do You Know?

Give the students the What do you know? page for Lessons 131-135. Tell them that this page will be used to see what they already know about the Words for the Week. Ask them to listen carefully to each word as you say it, repeat it in a sentence, and say it once again. Follow the procedures for this page as described in the *Introduction* at the beginning of this Teacher's Guide.

Ask the children to write their Working Words for the week in the word box and on their own paper.

Show the children how to write their Working Words in the appropriate section at the back of their *Spelling Dictionary.*

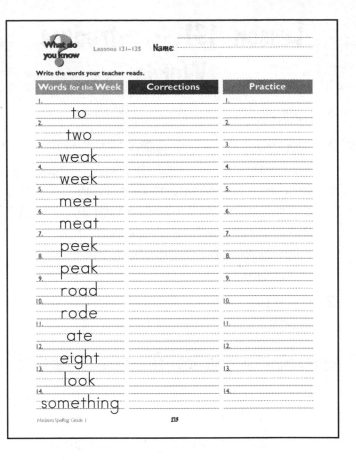

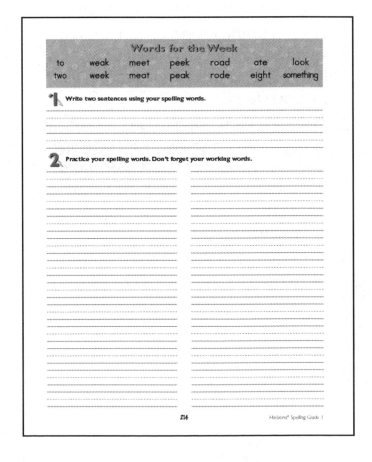

Lesson 131 - Introduce Words

Activities:

1. Give the students Lesson 131. Since homophones are tied directly to meaning, reinforce the meaning of each word and the need to remember the meaning and the correct spelling. Work with the children to match the words to the pictures in Activity 1.

2. Have the children write their Working Words on the lines provided.

Extended Activities for the Week:

1. Reproducible *Week 27 Worksheet* for in-class or take-home use.

   Make a word family page for homophones.

   Add to number word family page.

   Work with the children, or instruct parents to work with the children, to identify as many words as they can think of for each family.

2. Make a class word family chart for each family listed on the worksheet. Hang where children can see it. Add words as they are learned. Highlight or check off words that are part of spelling lessons or reading lessons.

3. Write sentences with the Working Words chosen for the week.

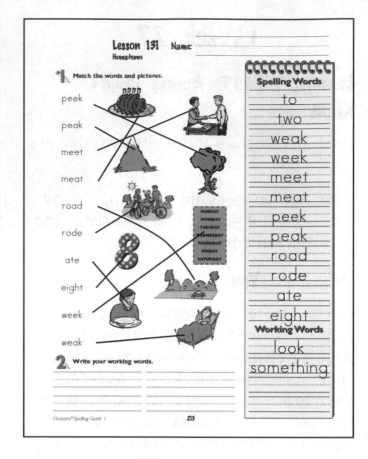

Lesson 132 - Examine and Explore Words

Teaching Tip:

Review spelling and meaning of each spelling word.

Activities:

1. Give the students Lesson 132. Ask the children to find four spelling words that rhyme, and write the words on the lines provided.

   NOTE: Any two rhyming pairs are acceptable. Suggested answers are given.

2. The second activity will help reinforce the use and meaning of the homophones. Have the children read the first sentence. Ask them to decide which pair of words is needed to complete the sentence. Ask them which spelling of the word is needed in each case. Check to see that they have written the correct homophone in the correct space. Repeat this process for the remaining sentences.

   NOTE: Remind the children that sentence Number 7 uses the two Working Words.

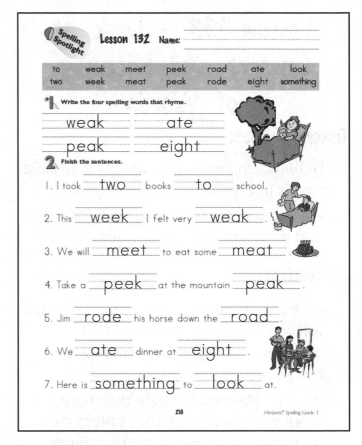

Extended Activities:

1. Make homophone word cards with pictures on them. Have the children take turns quizzing each other on the different spellings and meanings.

2. Add to homophone word family page.

3. Continue assembling word family pages into a booklet or binder.

Lesson 133 - Look at Context and Meaning of Words

Teaching Tips:

1. Help the children to locate their spelling words in the *Spelling Dictionary*.

2. Review spelling words, Working Words, and meanings of homophones.

Activities:

1. Give the students Lesson 133. This page will continue to reinforce the meaning/spelling relationship of the homophones in this unit.

2. Review crossword puzzle directions. Work this puzzle together unless children are able to work independently.

3. In Activity 2, tell the children that they will rearrange the words in each word box to make a sentence. Since these sentences are long, provide word cards for children having difficulty visualizing the sentences. Remind them to put a period at the end of the sentence.

Extended Activities:

1. Provide additional scrambled sentence practice if needed.

2. Drill meaning/spelling of homophones as needed.

Lesson 134 - Apply Understanding of Words in Writing

Teaching Tip:

Review spelling words, Working Words, and homophone meanings.

Activities:

1. Give the students Lesson 134. Read the story of the Good Samaritan to the children. Discuss the story. Ask the children ways in which they can be good Samaritans to others. Write any words on the board that may be needed for the writing assignment.

2. Ask the children to write a story about a time when they were (or when they could be) Good Samaritans to someone else.

3. Ask them to draw a picture to go with their story.

Lesson 134   Name: _____

Bible Story: *The Good Samaritan – Luke 10:30–37.*
Draw a picture and write a story telling how you can be a Good Samaritan.

I am a Good Samaritan when I _____

218   *Horizons® Spelling Grade 1*

Extended Activities:

1. Share stories and pictures with the class.

2. Have the children act out or illustrate the Bible story.

3. Review meaning/spelling of homophones.

Lesson 135 - Assess and Evaluate Progress

Activities:

1. Give the students Lesson 135. Tell the children that this is a "Check-up" page to see what they have learned during the week. [Note: Teachers/parents of home schoolers may decide what will be assessed. If a child did exceptionally well on the "What do you know?" pre-assessment, the teacher may choose not to test words already known by the child. Or the teacher may choose to test all Words for the Week.]

2. Tell the children that you will say a word. They will listen to the word and to the sentence you will give them. Then, they will write the word on the line next to the numbers. [Lines are given for the weekly words, but make sure to also check the Working Words for the week.]

3. Say the word. Repeat it in the context of a sentence. Repeat the word.

4. The children write the word dictated in the **Test** column.

5. The process is repeated until all words have been tested.

6. The teacher may correct in class by writing the words on the board and having the children compare or "self-correct" their work. Or the teacher may correct each child's work individually.

7. The teacher then uses the **Correction** column to write any corrections for words misspelled.

8. In the **Practice** column, the child copies the correct spelling of any words missed.

9. The second side of the page can be used for retesting, for testing additional sight or "Working Words" added for the week, and for additional practice.

Extended Activity:

Review any words missed.

Week 28

Lessons 136-140: Assess Child's Knowledge

Goal: To recognize and spell **ar** and **or** words.

Rule: An **r** after a vowel makes the vowel sound different from a short or long sound. Examples: **corn**, **for**, **born**, **are**, **far**, **barn**, **hard**, **part**, **car**.

What Do You Know?

Give the students the What do you know? page for Lessons 136-140. Tell them that this page will be used to see what they already know about the Words for the Week. Ask them to listen carefully to each word as you say it, repeat it in a sentence, and say it once again. Follow the procedures for this page as described in the *Introduction* at the beginning of this Teacher's Guide.

Ask the children to write their Working Words for the week in the word box and on their own paper.

Show the children how to write their Working Words in the appropriate section at the back of their *Spelling Dictionary*.

Lesson 136 - Introduce Words

Activities:

1. Give the students Lesson 136. Review the spelling words in the box. Ask the children to identify the pictures in Activity 1. On the line provided, ask them to write the spelling word that goes with each picture.

2. In Activity 2, ask the children to perform the following tasks:

   a. Find the correct shape for each word.

   b. Draw a line from the word to the shape.

   c. Write the word in the shape.

3. Write Working Words on the lines provided.

Extended Activities for the Week:

1. Reproducible *Week 28 Worksheet* for in-class or take-home use.

   Make word family pages for **ar** and **or**.

   Work with the children, or instruct parents to work with the children, to identify as many words as they can think of for each family.

2. Make a class word family chart for each family listed on the worksheet. Hang where children can see it. Add words as they are learned. Highlight or check off words that are part of spelling lessons or reading lessons.

3. Write sentences with the Working Words chosen for the week.

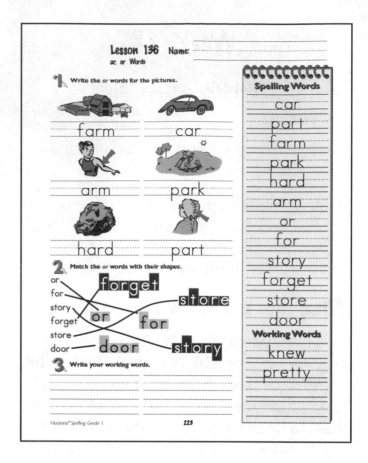

Horizons Spelling Grade 1

Lesson 137 - Examine and Explore Words

Teaching Tip:

Review spelling words, Working Words, and sentence rules.

Activities:

1. Give the students Lesson 137. Review rules for sentences: capital letters, punctuation.
2. Ask the children to write a sentence for each set of words.
3. Check and share sentences.

Extended Activities:

1. Have children work in pairs. Have each child select two spelling words and give them to his/her partner. The partner must spell the words and use them in a sentence. Repeat process for partner.
2. Add to word family pages.

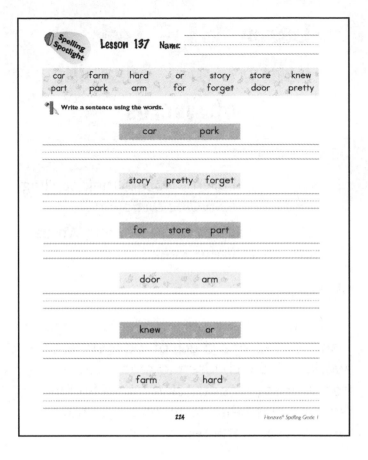

Lesson 138 - Look at Context and Meaning of Words

Teaching Tips:

1. Help the children to locate their spelling words in the *Spelling Dictionary*.

2. Review spelling words, Working Words, and rules for the week.

Activity:

Give the students Lesson 138. This page can be used as a check of independent work. Ask the children to read each sentence or statement. Ask them to find the spelling word that completes the statement and write it in the space. Check.

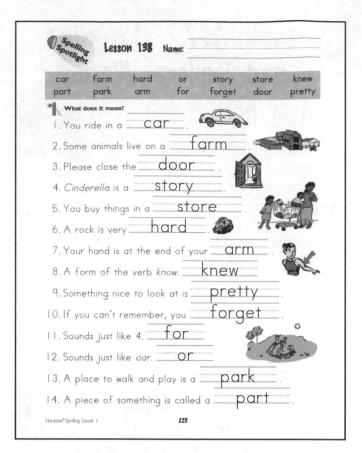

Extended Activities:

1. Review any concepts missed in the activity on this page.

2. Have children think of questions or definitions to be used with spelling words. Have each child present one question or definition for the class to guess.

Lesson 139 - Apply Understanding of Words in Writing

Teaching Tip:

Review spelling words, Working Words, and Bible stories.

Activities:

1. Give the students Lesson 139. Read and discuss the meaning of the word **parable**.

2. Read the parable from Matthew of the Wise and Foolish Virgins. Talk about how we can keep our hearts, our oil jars, full so that we are ready for Jesus.

3. Review the other parables listed in the word box. As you review, make a list of words on the board for each one of words that the children may need to complete the assignment.

4. Ask the children to choose one of the parables listed in the box. Have them draw a picture to fit the parable. Ask them to write about the story in the parable they chose and the lesson Jesus wanted us to learn from that story.

Lesson 139 Name: _____

Bible Story: *Jesus Uses a Story to Teach* – Matthew 25:1–13.
A parable is a story that teaches us a lesson. Jesus told many parables to teach us how to live. You have learned many parables this year. Pick one from the box or another favorite and tell about it. Draw a picture.

| The Good Shepherd | The Lost Sheep |
| The Good Samaritan | The Wise and Foolish Virgins |

228

Horizons® Spelling Grade 1

Extended Activities:

1. Share stories and pictures.

2. Act out or retell the parables.

3. Review spelling and Working Words for the week.

Lesson 140 - Assess and Evaluate Progress

Activities:

1. Give the students Lesson 140. Tell the children that this is a "Check-up" page to see what they have learned during the week. [Note: Teachers/parents of home schoolers may decide what will be assessed. If a child did exceptionally well on the "What do you know?" pre-assessment, the teacher may choose not to test words already known by the child. Or the teacher may choose to test all Words for the Week.]

2. Tell the children that you will say a word. They will listen to the word and to the sentence you will give them. Then, they will write the word on the line next to the numbers. [Lines are given for the weekly words, but make sure to also check the Working Words for the week.]

3. Say the word. Repeat it in the context of a sentence. Repeat the word.

4. The children write the word dictated in the **Test** column.

5. The process is repeated until all words have been tested.

6. The teacher may correct in class by writing the words on the board and having the children compare or "self-correct" their work. Or the teacher may correct each child's work individually.

7. The teacher then uses the **Correction** column to write any corrections for words misspelled.

8. In the **Practice** column, the child copies the correct spelling of any words missed.

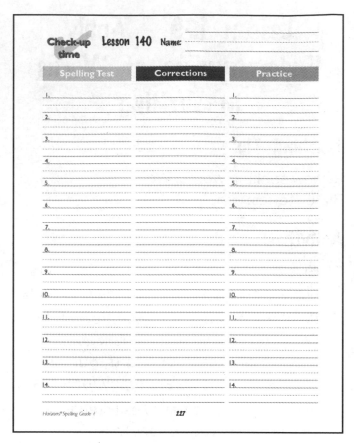

9. The second side of the page can be used for retesting, for testing additional sight or "Working Words" added for the week, and for additional practice.

Extended Activity:

Review any words missed.

Week 29

Lessons 141-145: Assess Child's Knowledge

Goal: To recognize and spell **ir**, **er**, and **ur** words.

Rule: An **r** after a vowel makes the vowel sound different from a short or long sound. Examples: **her**, **clerk**, **letter**, **first**, **dirt**, **skirt**, **nurse**, **fur**, **burn**.

What Do You Know?

Give the students the What do you know? page for Lessons 141-145. Tell them that this page will be used to see what they already know about the Words for the Week. Ask them to listen carefully to each word as you say it, repeat it in a sentence, and say it once again. Follow the procedures for this page as described in the *Introduction* at the beginning of this Teacher's Guide.

Ask the children to write their Working Words for the week in the word box and on their own paper.

Show the children how to write their Working Words in the appropriate section at the back of their *Spelling Dictionary*.

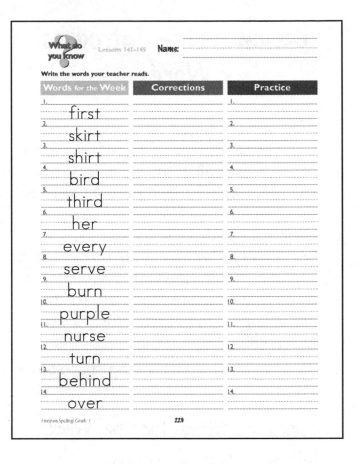

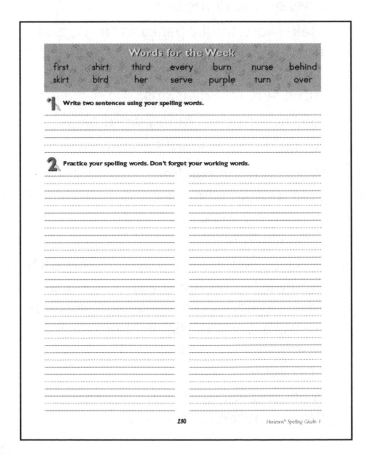

Lesson 141 - Introduce Words

Activities:

1. Give the students Lesson 141. Have the children read all of the spelling words. Ask them what three different spellings they see and hear for the same sound: **ir**, **er**, **ur**. Ask them to look at the first box. Read the words in the box. Ask the children to trace the words and to draw a line to the picture that matches the word. Repeat the process for the second word box.

2. Write Working Words in the space provided.

Extended Activities for the Week:

1. Reproducible *Week 29 Worksheet* for in-class or take-home use.

   Make word family pages for **ir**, **er**, and **ur**. Since all have the same sound, they could be part of the same page with three separate divisions.

   Add to "position" family word page.

   Add to number word family page.

   Work with the children, or instruct parents to work with the children, to identify as many words as they can think of for each family.

2. Make a class word family chart for each family listed on the worksheet. Hang where children can see it. Add words as they are learned. Highlight or check off words that are part of spelling lessons or reading lessons.

3. Write sentences with the Working Words chosen for the week.

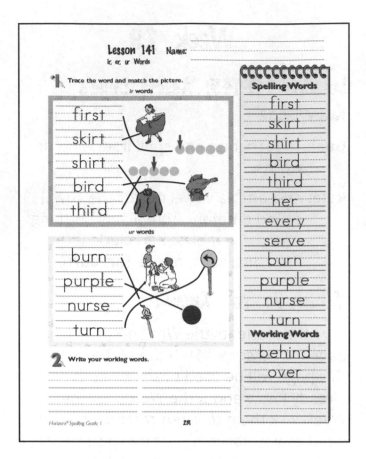

Lesson 142 - Examine and Explore Words

Teaching Tip:

Review spelling words, Working Words, and **r**-control rule.

Activities:

1. Give the students Lesson 142. Ask the children to find all the words in which the **er** spelling is found. Have them write the words on the lines provided.

2. In Activity 2, ask the children to unscramble each spelling word and write it on the line.

Extended Activities:

1. Have the children select 10 spelling words and use them in sentences.

2. Add to word family pages and charts. Continue to assemble word family book.

Lesson 143 - Look at Context and Meaning of Words

Teaching Tips:

1. Help the children to locate their spelling words in the *Spelling Dictionary*.
2. Review spelling words, Working Words, and rules for the week.

Activities:

1. Give the students Lesson 143. Review the words in the word box. Ask the children to read the clue for each word, find the word, and write it in the space. Check.

2. Read the account from John as Jesus washes the feet of his disciples and asks us to serve each other. Discuss what he did, why it was important, and how the children can serve each other. Have them write a sentence telling how they can serve others.

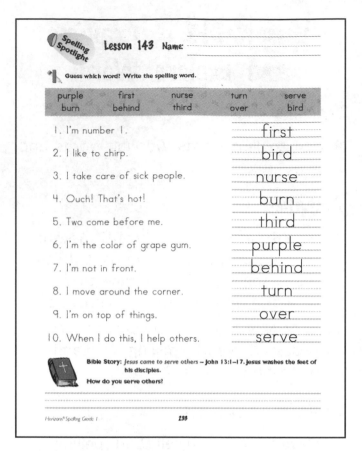

Extended Activities:

1. Share sentences about service.
2. Illustrate or recreate the Bible account.
3. Have children make up additional clues for the spelling words and quiz each other.

Lesson 144 - Apply Understanding of Words in Writing

Teaching Tip:

Review spelling words, Working Words, and Bible story.

Activities:

1. Give the students Lesson 144. Discuss the pictures with the children. Write any words on the board that may be needed for assignment.

2. Have the children complete the two paragraphs begun for them.

3. Check and share.

Extended Activity:

Review spelling and Working Words.

Lesson 144 Name: _____

The nurse serves us by _____

_____

_____

We should serve others by _____

_____

134

Horizons® Spelling Grade 1

Lesson 145 - Assess and Evaluate Progress

Activities:

1. Give the students Lesson 145. Tell the children that this is a "Check-up" page to see what they have learned during the week. [Note: Teachers/parents of home schoolers may decide what will be assessed. If a child did exceptionally well on the "What do you know?" pre-assessment, the teacher may choose not to test words already known by the child. Or the teacher may choose to test all Words for the Week.]

2. Tell the children that you will say a word. They will listen to the word and to the sentence you will give them. Then, they will write the word on the line next to the numbers. [Lines are given for the weekly words, but make sure to also check the Working Words for the week.]

3. Say the word. Repeat it in the context of a sentence. Repeat the word.

4. The children write the word dictated in the **Test** column.

5. The process is repeated until all words have been tested.

6. The teacher may correct in class by writing the words on the board and having the children compare or "self-correct" their work. Or the teacher may correct each child's work individually.

7. The teacher then uses the **Correction** column to write any corrections for words misspelled.

8. In the **Practice** column, the child copies the correct spelling of any words missed.

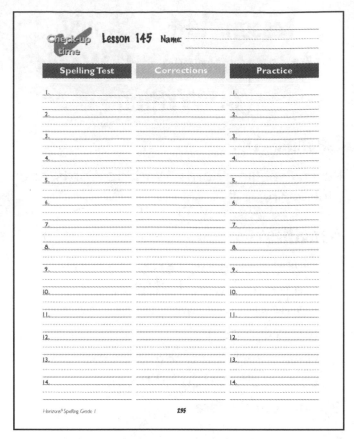

9. The second side of the page can be used for retesting, for testing additional sight or "Working Words" added for the week, and for additional practice.

Extended Activity:

Review any words missed.

Week 30

Lessons 146-150: Assess Child's Knowledge

Goal: To recognize and spell words with these sounds: **qu**, **ph**, **gh**, **igh**, and **ould**.

Rule: The letters **qu** stand for the **kw** sound.

Rule: The letters **ph** and **gh** can stand for the **f** sound.

Rule: Digraph **gh** can make two sounds. The **gh** can be silent. Examples: **right**, **night**. Gh can also make the **f** sound. Examples: **laugh**, **rough**, **tough**, **phone**, **elephant**.

What Do You Know?

Give the students the What do you know? page for Lessons 146-150. Tell them that this page will be used to see what they already know about the Words for the Week. Ask them to listen carefully to each word as you say it, repeat it in a sentence, and say it once again. Follow the procedures for this page as described in the *Introduction* at the beginning of this Teacher's Guide.

Ask the children to write their Working Words for the week in the word box and on their own paper.

Show the children how to write their Working Words in the appropriate section at the back of their *Spelling Dictionary.*

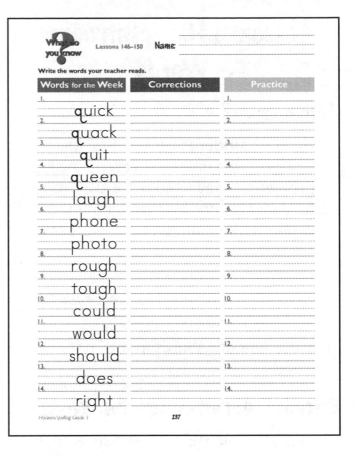

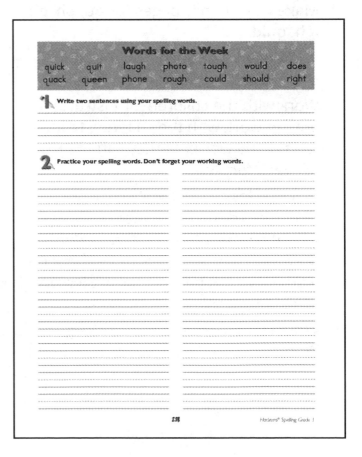

Lesson 146 - Introduce Words

Activities:

1. Give the students Lesson 146. Many words in this unit can present spelling problems. They need to be studied carefully and reinforced throughout the week so that children remember the spellings.

2. Help the children to sort the words and write them under the correct headings in the first activity.

3. Write Working Words in the space provided.

Extended Activities for the Week:

1. Reproducible *Week 30 Worksheet* for in-class or take-home use.

   Make word family pages for **qu**, **ph**, **gh**, **igh**, **ould**.

   Add the words **rough**, **tough** to the short **ŭ** page as well.

   Work with the children, or instruct parents to work with the children, to identify as many words as they can think of for each family.

2. Make a class word family chart for each family listed on the worksheet. Hang where children can see it. Add words as they are learned. Highlight or check off words that are part of spelling lessons or reading lessons.

3. Write sentences with the Working Words chosen for the week.

Name: Milli   12/14 = 86%

1 Should ✓   11 quick ✓
2 could ✓   12 quick ✓
3 Would ✓   13 dose ✗ does
4 tough ✓   14 right ✓
5 photo ✓
6 rough ✓
7 queen ✓
8 lagh ✗ Laugh
9 phone ✓
10 quite ✗ quit

Lesson 147 - Examine and Explore Words

Teaching Tip:

Review spelling words and specific spelling problems.

Activity:

Give the students Lesson 147. Do this puzzle together in class. Check spelling and placement of words.

Extended Activities:

1. Add to word family charts.
2. Have children quiz each other on the spelling of the words in this unit.

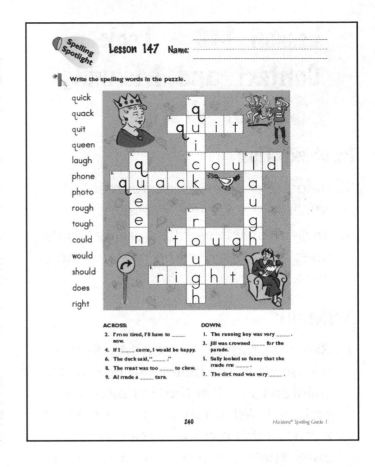

Lesson 148 - Look at Context and Meaning of Words

Teaching Tips:

1. Help the children to locate their spelling words in the *Spelling Dictionary*.
2. Review spelling words, Working Words, rules for sentences and rules for the week.

Activities:

1. Give the students Lesson 148. Review the words in the blue word box. Ask the children to look at the first picture in Activity 1. Ask them to use the spelling word for this picture, **queen**, and any other spelling words they can in a sentence. Repeat process for the remaining pictures.
2. Read the story of Queen Esther to the children. Talk about how brave she was, how she trusted totally in God, and how she saved her people. Select a verse or two from the story for the children to learn.

Extended Activities:

1. Have the children draw and write or act out part of the story of Queen Esther.
2. Use any spelling words not used in the first activity in sentences.

Lesson 149 - Apply Understanding of Words in Writing

Teaching Tip:

Review spelling words, Working Words, rules, and sentence structure.

Activities:

1. Give the students Lesson 149. Read the directions to the children. Brainstorm ideas for the story they are to write. See how many spelling words they can use in their stories.

2. Ask the children to write their stories and then to draw a picture of one of the funny things the king did to make the queen laugh.

Extended Activities:

1. Share stories. Select one or two to act out for the class.

2. Add any misspelled words to the child's individual list of words to study.

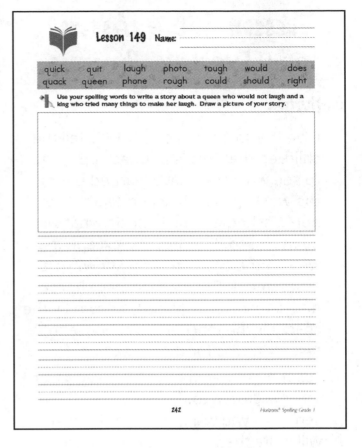

Lesson 149 Name:

| quick | quit | laugh | photo | tough | would | does |
| quack | queen | phone | rough | could | should | right |

Use your spelling words to write a story about a queen who would not laugh and a king who tried many things to make her laugh. Draw a picture of your story.

242   Horizons® Spelling Grade 1

Lesson 150 - Assess and Evaluate Progress

Activities:

1. Give the students Lesson 150. Tell the children that this is a "Check-up" page to see what they have learned during the week. [Note: Teachers/parents of home schoolers may decide what will be assessed. If a child did exceptionally well on the "What do you know?" pre-assessment, the teacher may choose not to test words already known by the child. Or the teacher may choose to test all Words for the Week.]

2. Tell the children that you will say a word. They will listen to the word and to the sentence you will give them. Then, they will write the word on the line next to the numbers. [Lines are given for the weekly words, but make sure to also check the Working Words for the week.]

3. Say the word. Repeat it in the context of a sentence. Repeat the word.

4. The children write the word dictated in the **Test** column.

5. The process is repeated until all words have been tested.

6. The teacher may correct in class by writing the words on the board and having the children compare or "self-correct" their work. Or the teacher may correct each child's work individually.

7. The teacher then uses the **Correction** column to write any corrections for words misspelled.

8. In the **Practice** column, the child copies the correct spelling of any words missed.

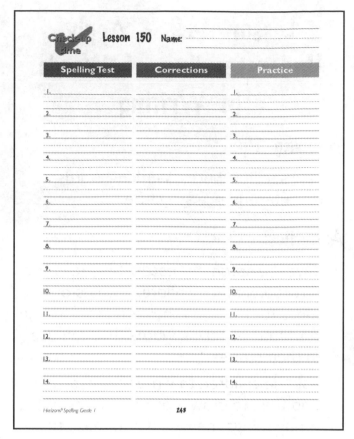

9. The second side of the page can be used for retesting, for testing additional sight or "Working Words" added for the week, and for additional practice.

Extended Activity:

Review any words missed.

Week 31

Lessons 151-155: Assess Child's Knowledge

Goal: To recognize and spell words ending in **–ed** and **–ing**.

Rule: If a word with a short vowel sound ends in a single consonant, usually double the consonant before adding a suffix that begins with a vowel. Examples: **run/running**; **dig/digging**; **tag/tagged, tagging**; **big/bigger, biggest**; **fat/fatter, fattest**.

Rule: If a word ends in silent **e**, drop the **e** before adding a suffix that begins with a vowel. Examples: **bake/baking**, **write/writer**, **slice/slicing**.

What Do You Know?

Give the students the What do you know? page for Lessons 151-155. Tell them that this page will be used to see what they already know about the Words for the Week. Ask them to listen carefully to each word as you say it, repeat it in a sentence, and say it once again. Follow the procedures for this page as described in the *Introduction* at the beginning of this Teacher's Guide.

Ask the children to write their Working Words for the week in the word box and on their own paper.

Show the children how to write their Working Words in the appropriate section at the back of their *Spelling Dictionary*.

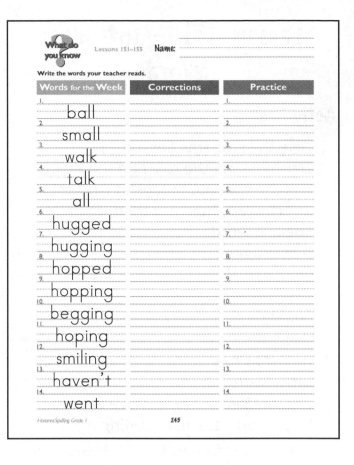

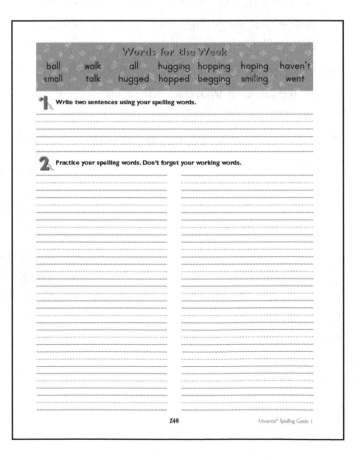

Lesson 151 - Introduce Words

Activities:

1. Give the students Lesson 151. Demonstrate the rules on the board. Ask the children to look at the first word in Activity 1, **hug**. Ask them to find two spelling words that contain the word **hug** (**hugged, hugging**). Ask the children what was done to the base word hug so that the endings (suffixes) **–ed, –ing** could be added. Have them write the two words on the lines provided below the word **hug**. Repeat the process for other words in the first activity. Note that the second rule above applies to **hope/hoping, smile/smiling**.

2. Ask the children to find and write the contraction haven't on the line for Activity 2. Ask them what two words were put together to form the contraction. Write them on the board.

3. In Activity 3, ask the children to find and write all the words that have the al sound.

4. Write Working Words on the lines provided.

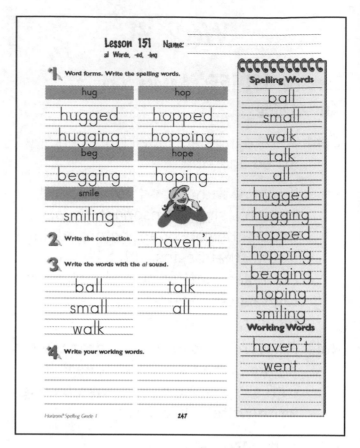

Extended Activities for the Week:

1. Reproducible *Week 31 Worksheet* for in-class or take-home use.

   Make word family pages that demonstrate the rules given.

   These will be the last pages in the booklet for this year.

   Work with the children, or instruct parents to work with the children, to identify as many words as they can think of for each family.

2. Make a class word family chart for each family listed on the worksheet. Hang where children can see it. Add words as they are learned. Highlight or check off words that are part of spelling lessons or reading lessons.

3. Write sentences with the Working Words chosen for the week.

Lesson 152 - Examine and Explore Words

Teaching Tip:

Review rules, spelling words, and Working Words.

Activities:

1. Give the students Lesson 152. Activity 1 reinforces the rules for this week's lessons. Read with the children or allow them to work independently as they are able. Check together.

2. In Activity 2, as the children to find all the spelling words in the box that rhyme with the first word in the line. Have them write the words.

Extended Activities:

1. Give additional practice in adding suffixes to words not in this unit: **dig**, **tag**, **pop**, **mop**, etc; **bake**, **slice**, **mope**, etc.

2. Choose 10 spelling words and write them in sentences.

3. Complete word family pages for this week.

Lesson 153 - Look at Context and Meaning of Words

Teaching Tips:

1. Help the children to locate their spelling words in the *Spelling Dictionary*.
2. Review spelling words, Working Words, and rules for the week.

Activities:

1. Give the students Lesson 153. The first activity on this page will allow assessment of the children's grasp of the rules for this week. Ask the children to read the sentences carefully, to look very closely at the word choices, and to select the word that will complete each sentence. Ask them to circle their choices. Check and make corrections as needed BEFORE they write the words in the spaces provided.
2. Read the Bible story to the children. Talk about what Jesus did. Ask the children to think about what it would be like to be blind, then suddenly, be able to see.

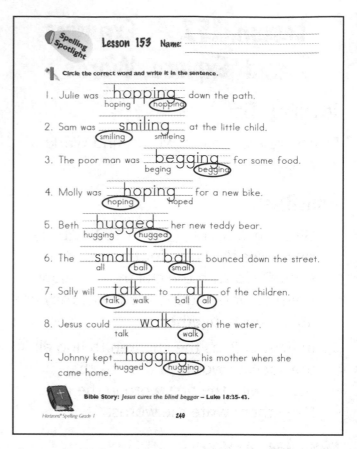

Extended Activities:

1. Review and provide additional practice for any words in the first activity that confuse the children.
2. Have the children draw and write about the story of the blind beggar.
3. Have the children present a play about the Bible story.

Lesson 154 - Apply Understanding of Words in Writing

Teaching Tip:

Review rules, spelling words, and Working Words.

Activities:

1. Give the students Lesson 154. Read the directions with the children. Talk about things they might see in the park. If there is a park nearby, visit it before completing this activity.

2. Ask the children to write their own stories about a walk in the park.

3. Have them complete the drawing with the details they have put in their stories.

Extended Activities:

1. Share stories.

2. Review words as needed.

Lesson 154   Name: _____

Study the picture. Write a story about what you might see as you walk through the park. Finish the picture with things in your story.

A Walk in the Park

250   *Horizons® Spelling Grade 1*

Lesson 155 - Assess and Evaluate Progress

Activities:

1. Give the students Lesson 155. Tell the children that this is a "Check-up" page to see what they have learned during the week. [Note: Teachers/parents of home schoolers may decide what will be assessed. If a child did exceptionally well on the "What do you know?" pre-assessment, the teacher may choose not to test words already known by the child. Or the teacher may choose to test all Words for the Week.]

2. Tell the children that you will say a word. They will listen to the word and to the sentence you will give them. Then, they will write the word on the line next to the numbers. [Lines are given for the weekly words, but make sure to also check the Working Words for the week.]

3. Say the word. Repeat it in the context of a sentence. Repeat the word.

4. The children write the word dictated in the **Test** column.

5. The process is repeated until all words have been tested.

6. The teacher may correct in class by writing the words on the board and having the children compare or "self-correct" their work. Or the teacher may correct each child's work individually.

7. The teacher then uses the **Correction** column to write any corrections for words misspelled.

8. In the **Practice** column, the child copies the correct spelling of any words missed.

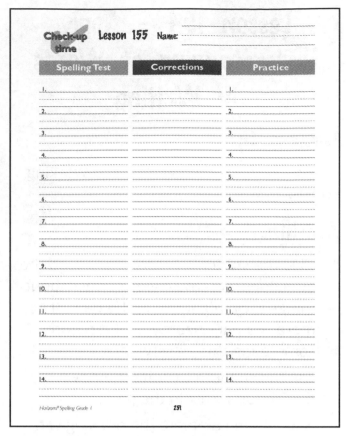

9. The second side of the page can be used for retesting, for testing additional sight or "Working Words" added for the week, and for additional practice.

Extended Activity:

Review any words missed.

Week 32

Lessons 156-160: Assess Child's Knowledge

Goal: To review spelling words from Lessons 117–155.

What Do You Remember?

Give the students the What do you remember? page for Lessons 117-155. Tell them that this page will be used to see what they remember about the words they have studied so far this year. Select an additional four to six Working Words from the list of words added each week. Ask them to listen carefully to each word as you say it, repeat it in a sentence, and say it once again. Follow the procedures for this page as described in the *Introduction* at the beginning of this Teacher's Guide.

NOTE: If you have kept records of words that each child continues to find difficult, you may want to adjust the words in this unit to fit the needs of the individual child. Replace review words already mastered with those still needing work.

What do you remember — Lessons 117-155   Name: _____

Write the words your teacher reads.

1.	13.	25.
2. happy	14. pretty	26. went
3. many	15. knew	27. haven't
4. with	16. for	28. all
5. kind	17. story	smiling
6. always	18. over	
7. never	19. behind	
8. little	20. every	
9. more	21. first	
10. something	22. right	
11. to	23. quick	
12. two	24. would	
eight	should	

Horizons Spelling Grade 1   153

Review Words

happy	always	something	pretty	over	right	went
many	never	to	knew	behind	quick	haven't
with	little	two	for	every	would	all
kind	more	eight	story	first	should	smiling

Practice your review words.

154   Horizons® Spelling Grade 1

Horizons Spelling Grade 1   **209**

Lesson 156 - Introduce Words

Activities:

1. Give the students Lesson 156. The activities in this week's lessons may be used as independent assessment of concepts. Read the directions for Activity 1. Ask the children to complete. Check.

2. Read the directions for Activity 2. Make sure children understand the words given in the list so that they can find and write the spelling word for the opposite concept.

Extended Activities for the Week:

1. Use the sheets, charts, or booklets created for the word family exercises to help the children review all the words studied to date, not simply those included in the lesson. Include all Working Words given in the weeks prior to this one.

2. Have the children use the review spelling words in sentences.

3. Complete word family booklets and charts for the year.

4. Reproducible *Week 32 Worksheet* for in-class or take-home use.

Lesson 157 - Examine and Explore Words

Activities:

1. Give the students Lesson 157. Read the directions for Activity 1. Ask the children to put the review spelling words in the green box into ABC order. Check.

2. Ask the children to look at the review spelling words in the bordered box. Ask the children to perform the following tasks:

   a. Find the correct shape for each word.

   b. Draw a line from the word to the shape.

   c. Write the word in the shape.

Extended Activities:

1. Review ABC order if needed.

2. Complete word family booklets.

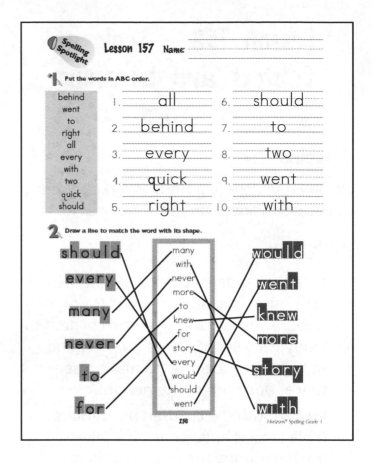

Lesson 158 - Look at Context and Meaning of Words

Teaching Tip:

Review rules, spelling words, Working Words, punctuation and sentence structure.

Activities:

1. Give the students Lesson 158. Review sentence structure and rules for capitalization with children. Ask the children to study each set of words carefully and put each set together to make a sentence. Don't forget the period!

2. Review with the children the various Bible stories and verses they have learned during the year. Ask them to write a sentence about their favorite.

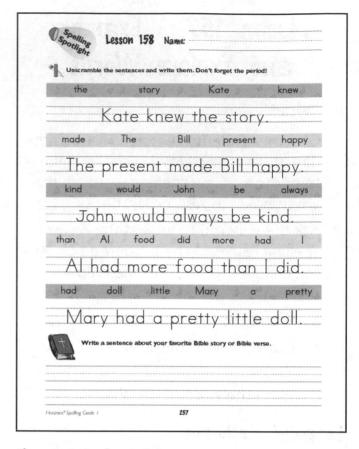

Extended Activities:

1. Provide additional sentence practice as needed.

2. Share sentences about Bible verses.

Lesson 159 - Apply Understanding of Words in Writing

Teaching Tips:

1. Review spelling words, Working Words, and rules.
2. Have *Spelling Dictionary* at hand and have the children look at all the words they have learned this year, both in the printed section of the dictionary and in their own written section.

Activities:

1. Give the students Lesson 159. Read the directions. Share some ideas about this year in first grade. Ask the children to write their own story about what they have learned.
2. Have them draw a picture of themselves.

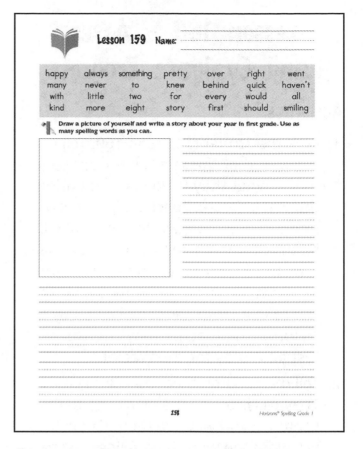

Extended Activities:

1. Share stories and pictures.
2. Review any concepts still needing reinforcement.

Lesson 160 - Assess and Evaluate Progress

Activities:

1. Give the students Lesson 160. Tell the children that this is a "Check-up" page to see what they have learned during the week. [Note: Teachers/parents of home schoolers may decide what will be assessed. If a child did exceptionally well on the "What do you know?" pre-assessment, the teacher may choose not to test words already known by the child. Or the teacher may choose to test all Words for the Week.]

2. Tell the children that you will say a word. They will listen to the word and to the sentence you will give them. Then, they will write the word on the line next to the numbers. [Lines are given for the weekly words, but make sure to also check the Working Words for the week.]

3. Say the word. Repeat it in the context of a sentence. Repeat the word.

4. The children write the word dictated in the **Test** column.

5. The process is repeated until all words have been tested.

6. The teacher may correct in class by writing the words on the board and having the children compare or "self-correct" their work. Or the teacher may correct each child's work individually.

7. The teacher then uses the **Correction** column to write any corrections for words misspelled.

8. In the **Practice** column, the child copies the correct spelling of any words missed.

9. The second side of the page can be used for retesting, for testing additional sight or "Working Words" added for the week, and for additional practice.

Extended Activity:

Review any words missed.

Check-up time Lesson 160 Name:

Write the words your teacher reads.

1. 13. 25.
2. 14. 26.
3. 15. 27.
4. 16. 28.
5. 17.
6. 18.
7. 19.
8. 20.
9. 21.
10. 22.
11. 23.
12. 24.

Horizons Spelling Grade 1 **159**

Reproducible Worksheets

Week 1 Worksheet
Short ă & ĕ Practice

_____

1. Say the name of the picture. Circle the pictures for short ă words. Write the short ă words on the lines.

Word List

hat

can

bat

cat

_____ _____ _____ _____

2. Say the name of the picture. Circle the pictures for short ĕ words. Write the short ĕ words on the lines.

Word List

net

hen

bell

jet

_____ _____ _____ _____

Week 2 Worksheet
Short ĭ & ŏ Practice

Cut and paste the short ĭ and short ŏ words in the correct row.

Short ĭ words

Short ŏ words

will	hop	on
not	did	is
his	God	mom

Week 3 Worksheet
Soft c & g Practice

Look at the pictures. Draw a circle around the pictures that begin with soft c.
Draw a square around the pictures that begin with soft g.

Word List

cent

giraffe

circus

gem

circle

giant

city

Week 4 Worksheet
Long ā Practice

Which spelling is it? Find the correct spelling of long ā to complete these spelling words. Cut out the spelling and paste it on the line.

d _____   g _____ te

r _____ n   s _____ l

s _____   c _____ ke

m _____ ke   m _____ l

pl _____ ce   m _____ de

ay	a	a	ai	ai
ay	a	a	a	ai

Week 5 Worksheet
Long ē Practice

_____
- -
_____

 Draw lines to match the words and pictures. Write the words on the lines.

bee

beet

heel

key

knee

kneel

meat

seal

street

wheat

_____ _____ _____ _____
- - - - - - - - - - - - - - - - - - - - - - - - - - - - - - - - - - - - - - - -
_____ _____ _____ _____
- - - - - - - - - - - - - - - - - - - - - - - - - - - - - - - - - - - - - - - -
_____ _____ _____ _____

          _____ _____
          - - - - - - - - - - - - - - - - - - - -
          _____ _____

Week 6 Worksheet
Sentences

_____
- - - - - - - - - - - - - - - - - -
_____

Complete the sentences. Cut out the correct word and paste it on the line.

1. _____ name is _____ .
   (Write your name here.)

2. Can you see _____ ?

3. _____ love to spell.

4. This is _____ paper.

5. This pencil is _____ .

6. _____ go to school.

7. These crayons are _____ .

8. Come with _____ .

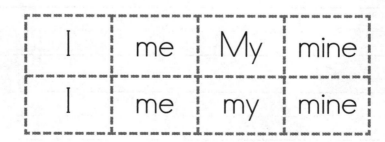

I	me	My	mine
I	me	my	mine

Week 7 Worksheet
Long ō words spelled with oa

_____

- - - - - - - - - - - - - - - - - - -

_____

✏ Finish each line with a word from the Word List.
Hint: One word will be used 2 times. Draw a picture for your rhyme.

There once was a _____

Who sailed in a _____

That couldn't _____ .

He had a sore _____

So he put on a _____ .

He _____ a _____ .

That silly _____ !

Word List

note

goat

float

coat

boat

wrote

throat

Week 8 Worksheet
Sentences

Cut the cards apart and use them to review your spelling words.
Can you make sentences with these words?

said	were	Jesus
God	mother	father
they	the	and
have	but	home

Horizons Spelling Grade 1

Week 9 Worksheet
Crossword Puzzle Practice

Solve each crossword puzzle.

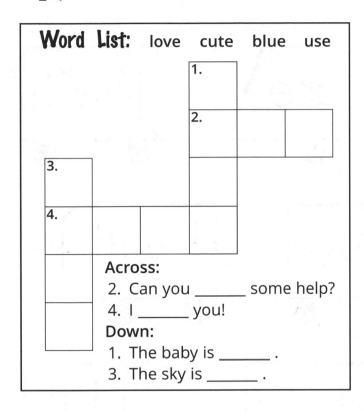

Word List: love   cute   blue   use

Across:
2. Can you _____ some help?
4. I _____ you!
Down:
1. The baby is _____ .
3. The sky is _____ .

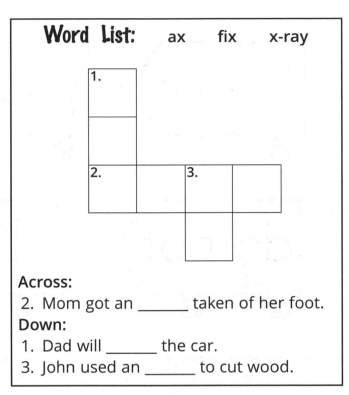

Word List: ax   fix   x-ray

Across:
2. Mom got an _____ taken of her foot.
Down:
1. Dad will _____ the car.
3. John used an _____ to cut wood.

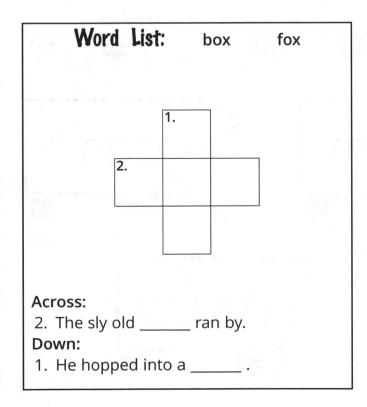

Word List: box   fox

Across:
2. The sly old _____ ran by.
Down:
1. He hopped into a _____ .

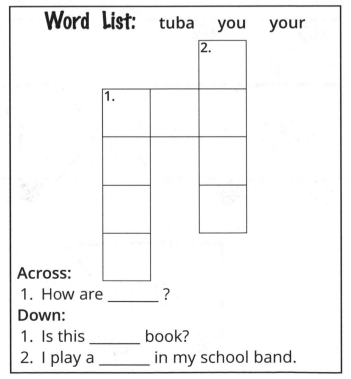

Word List: tuba   you   your

Across:
1. How are _____ ?
Down:
1. Is this _____ book?
2. I play a _____ in my school band.

Week 10 Worksheet
Contractions

  Cut and paste together the pieces for this "Contraction Train."

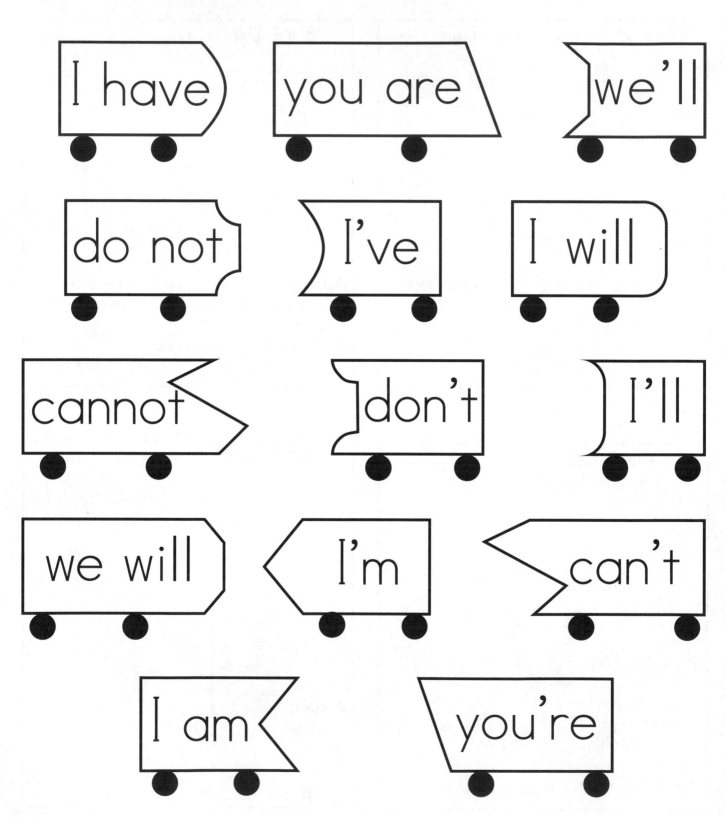

Horizons Spelling Grade 1

Week 11 Worksheet
Plurals

_____

- - - - - - - - - - - - - - - - -

_____

Add –s or –es. Write the words.

church _____

_____

- - - - - - - - - - - - - - - - -

_____

watch _____

- - - - - - - - - - - - - - - - -

_____

toy _____

- - - - - - - - - - - - - - - - -

_____

girl _____

- - - - - - - - - - - - - - - - -

_____

boy _____

- - - - - - - - - - - - - - - - -

_____

hunch _____

- - - - - - - - - - - - - - - - -

_____

wish _____

- - - - - - - - - - - - - - - - -

_____

pizza _____

- - - - - - - - - - - - - - - - -

_____

peg _____

- - - - - - - - - - - - - - - - -

_____

match _____

- - - - - - - - - - - - - - - - -

_____

Week 12 Worksheet
Comparisons

Write the missing words in each box.

| long | _____ | longest |

| _____ | faster | _____ |

| kind | kinder | _____ |

| _____ | _____ | highest |

| soft | _____ | _____ |

Week 13 Worksheet
Adding -ful, -ing, -ness

 Cut and paste the correct suffix beside each word.

fall   peace

soft   snow

grow   dark

cheer   cook

joy   truth

ful	ful	ing	ing	ness
ful	ful	ing	ing	ness

Week 14 Worksheet
ABC Order

Cut the cards out and line them up in alphabetical order.
Add one working word in the blank box.

Mr.	lamb	back
high	night	know
write	sign	gnat
climb	whole	Mrs.
light	knock	

Week 15 Worksheet

oo Sounds

✂ Cut out the word cards at the bottom of the page.
Paste them under the correct oo sound.

Book

Moon

| spoon | hook | pool | roof | cook |
| shook | toot | wood | goose | wool |

Week 16 Worksheet
Scrambled Sentences

Cut out each set of words and arrange them into a sentence.
Store them in an envelope to practice with them again.

playful	is	Your	puppy

now	words	I'm	faster	spelling

I	kindest	brother	have	My
the	friend	Jim	is	

love	other	Good	each	people

great	happiness	Jesus	us
and	gives	love	

Week 17 Worksheet
Complete the Sentences

_____
- -
_____

Use the words from the Word List to complete the sentences.

Word List

our	out	bowl	Paul	house
straw	about	saw	down	yellow

1. Saul's name was changed to _____ .

2. I had soup in a _____ _____ .

3. Did you hear _____ the party?

4. I _____ a big pile of _____ at Grandma's farm.

5. I ran _____ the stairs and _____ the door.

6. _____ car is green.

7. My friend lives in a big white _____ .

Week 18 Worksheet
More Compound Words

 Draw lines to connect the words and make compound words.
Match the compound words to the pictures.

bed   man

snow   dog

base   brush

air   room

hair   ball

hot   plane

 Write the compound words on the lines.

Week 19 Worksheet
More Sentence Practice

_____

Use each set of words in a sentence. You will have to add your own words to complete the sentence. Draw a picture to go with the sentence.

plant   six   green

_____

clock   brown   free

_____

five   fly   frog

_____

Use your Working Words for this sentence.

_____

Week 20 Worksheet
ABC Order Practice

_____

- - - - - - - - - - - - - - - - -

_____

Cut the word cards apart and arrange them in alphabetical order.
Write one working word in the blank card.

Easter	snail	sky
street	skip	snake
speak	after	smoke
smell	slip	stove
snow	stop	

Week 21 Worksheet
Sentence Practice

_____
- -
_____

✏ **Use each word in a sentence.**

there

them

their

this

that

then

she

ship

shoe

shall

Week 22 Worksheet
Crossword Fun

_____

- -

_____

1. Complete the crossword puzzle.

Across:
2. I had a sandwich for

   _____ .
3. The little _____ was
   happy.
4. Jesus loves little _____ .
6. I went to _____ today.
9. The dog ran to fetch
   the _____ .

Down:
1. We went to _____ on
   Sunday.
3. She fell and bumped
   her _____ .
5. Can you hear the
   _____ ?
7. Jesus is the _____ .
8. Don't forget to _____
   the door.

2. Write the spelling words for this week that were NOT used in this puzzle.

_____ _____

- - - - - - - - - - - - - - - - - - - - - - - - - -

_____ _____

238

Week 23 Worksheet
Plurals

1. Write the plurals of the words.

church _____   girl _____

watch _____   boy _____

toy _____   hunch _____

2. Choose a word from the Word List to complete the sentences.

Word List

who	what	when	where	which	whale

1. _____ saw the _____ ?

2. _____ will you show me _____ you put the books?

3. _____ time is it?

4. _____ dog is yours?

Week 24 Worksheet
Rhymes

Write two words that rhyme with each of the spelling words.

joy

stop

street

that

thank

for

house

sleep

pray

when

where

bless

Week 25 Worksheet
ABC Order

_____
- - - - - - - - - - - - - - - - - -
_____

Cut the cards apart and arrange them in alphabetical order.
Write a working word in the empty box.

happy	many	nice
gift	present	with
lass	boy	kind
toss	joyful	girl
throw	lad	

Week 26 Worksheet
More Opposites

 Draw a line to connect the words that are opposites.

boy   winter   wet   day

high   fast  light   she

summer   small   he   windy

large   girl  night   dry

slow   low   calm   dark

 Write the opposite word pairs on the lines below.

Horizons Spelling Grade 1

Week 27 Worksheet
More Homophones

 Complete the sentences by underlining the correct homophone.

1. (Won, One) day, John (won, one) a race.

2. Did you come here to (see, sea) the (see, sea) lions?

3. The wind (blue, blew) Mary's (blue, blew) hat off.

4. (Know, No) (won, one) (knew, new) the answer to the teacher's question.

5. (Eye, I) got some dust in my (eye, I).

6. At what (our, hour) will we be eating (our, hour) meal?

7. Matt looked (pale, pail) when he dropped the (pale, pail) of water.

8. Did you (here, hear) me call you over (here, hear)?

9. Last (night, knight) I read a story about a (night, knight).

10. Bill does (knot, not) (know, no) how to untie the (knot, not) in his shoelace.

11. Please (wait, weight) while I check my (wait, weight) on the scale.

12. (Eye, I) can (see, sea) the (see, sea) from my bedroom window.

_____

- -

_____

Draw a picture of your favorite activity (hiking, swimming, reading, camping, going to the zoo, etc.) and then write a story about your picture.

Week 29 Worksheet
Dictionary Work

_____
- -
_____

Look up these words in your Spelling Dictionary. Copy the sentence you find there on the first line. Write a new sentence of your own on the second line.

serve

Dictionary:_____

My sentence: _____

first

Dictionary:_____

My sentence: _____

shirt

Dictionary:_____

My sentence: _____

behind

Dictionary:_____

My sentence: _____

over

Dictionary:_____

My sentence: _____

bird

Dictionary:_____

My sentence: _____

burn

Dictionary:_____

My sentence: _____

purple

Dictionary:_____

My sentence: _____

Week 30 Worksheet
ABC Order

Cut the cards apart and arrange them in alphabetical order. Add the Worksheet 25 cards for a more challenging activity. Write a working word on the blank card.

quick	quack	quit
queen	phone	laugh
photo	rough	tough
could	does	right
would	should	

Week 31 Worksheet
Adding the Suffix -ing to Words

RULE: If a word with a short vowel ends in a single consonant, usually double the consonant before adding a suffix that begins with a vowel.

RULE: If a word ends in silent e, drop the e before adding a suffix that begins with a vowel.

 Using your rules for this week, add -ing to the following words. Write the words.

hit + ing = _____   win + ing = _____

skip + ing = _____   zip + ing = _____

get + ing = _____   mop + ing = _____

pop + ing = _____   rub + ing = _____

 Using your rules for this week, add -ing to the following words. Write the words.

rope + ing = _____   file + ing = _____

come + ing = _____   fake + ing = _____

love + ing = _____   hide + ing = _____

mine + ing = _____   wipe + ing = _____

wave + ing = _____   ride + ing = _____

Week 32 Worksheet
Final Sentence Practice

_____

_____

Use each set of words in a sentence.
You will have to add your own words to complete the sentence.

happy   pretty   smiling

_____

_____

_____

always   kind   went

_____

_____

_____

little   quick   every

_____

_____

_____

something   never   many

_____

_____

_____

Worksheets
Answer Keys

Key for Week 1 Worksheet

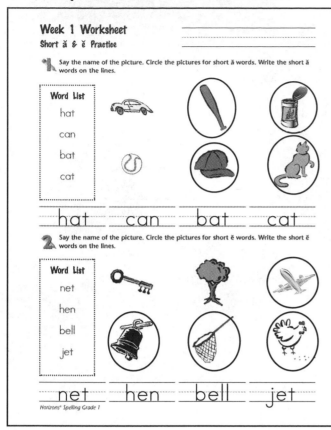

Week 1 Worksheet _____

Short ă & ĕ Practice

Say the name of the picture. Circle the pictures for short ă words. Write the short ă words on the lines.

Word List

hat
can
bat
cat

hat   can   bat   cat

Say the name of the picture. Circle the pictures for short ĕ words. Write the short ĕ words on the lines.

Word List

net
hen
bell
jet

net   hen   bell   jet

Horizons Spelling Grade 1

Key for Week 2 Worksheet

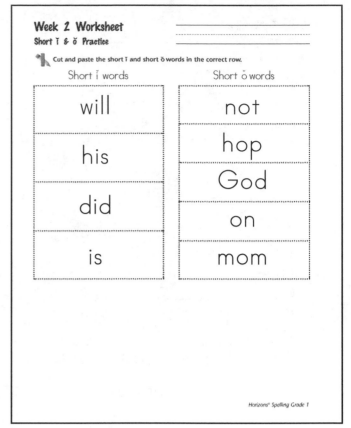

Week 2 Worksheet _____

Short ĭ & ŏ Practice

Cut and paste the short ĭ and short ŏ words in the correct row.

Short ĭ words	Short ŏ words
will	not
his	hop
did	God
is	on
	mom

Horizons Spelling Grade 1

Key for Week 3 Worksheet

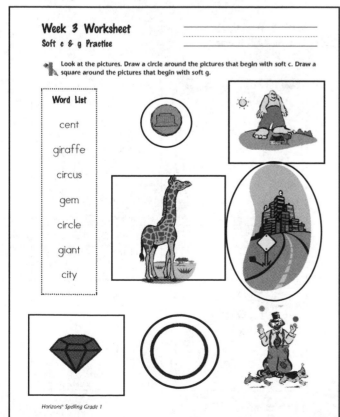

Week 3 Worksheet _____

Soft c & g Practice

Look at the pictures. Draw a circle around the pictures that begin with soft c. Draw a square around the pictures that begin with soft g.

Word List

cent
giraffe
circus
gem
circle
giant
city

Horizons Spelling Grade 1

Key for Week 4 Worksheet

Week 4 Worksheet _____

Long ā Practice

Which spelling is it? Find the correct spelling of long ā to complete these spelling words. Cut out the spelling and paste it on the line.

d __ay__   g __a__ te

r __ai__ n   s __ai__ l

s __ay__   c __a__ ke

m __a__ ke   m __ai__ l

pl __a__ ce   m __a__ de

Horizons Spelling Grade 1

Key for Week 5 Worksheet

Week 5 Worksheet _____
Long ē Practice _____

✂ Draw lines to match the words and pictures. Write the words on the lines.

bee
beet
heel
key
knee
kneel
meat
seal
street
wheat

bee	beet	heel	key
knee	kneel	meat	seal
	street	wheat	

Horizons® Spelling Grade 1

Key for Week 6 Worksheet

Week 6 Worksheet _____
Sentences _____

✂ Complete the sentences. Cut out the correct word and paste it on the line.

1. __My__ name is _____ .
   (Write your name here.)
2. Can you see ___me___ ?
3. __I__ love to spell.
4. This is ___my___ paper.
5. This pencil is ___mine___ .
6. ___I___ go to school.
7. These crayons are ___mine___ .
8. Come with ___me___ .

Horizons® Spelling Grade 1

Key for Week 7 Worksheet

Week 7 Worksheet _____
Long ō words spelled with oa _____

✂ Finish each line with a word from the word box. Hint: One word will be used 2 times. Draw a picture for your rhyme.

There once was a __goat__
Who sailed in a __boat__
That couldn't __float__ .
He had a sore __throat__
So he put on a __coat__ .
He __wrote__ a __note__ .
That silly __goat__ !

Word List

note
goat
float
coat
wrote
throat

Horizons® Spelling Grade 1

Key for Week 9 Worksheet

Week 9 Worksheet _____
Crossword Puzzle Practice _____

✂ Solve each crossword puzzle.

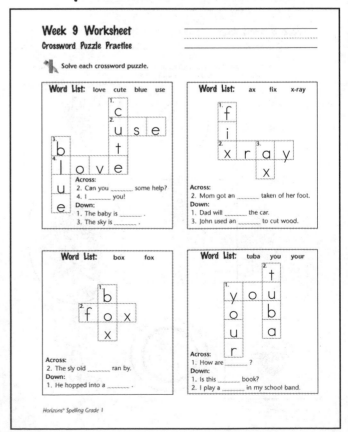

Word List: love cute blue use

Across:
2. Can you _____ some help?
4. I _____ you!
Down:
1. The baby is _____ .
3. The sky is _____ .

Word List: ax fix x-ray

Across:
2. Mom got an _____ taken of her foot.
Down:
1. Dad will _____ the car.
3. John used an _____ to cut wood.

Word List: box fox

Across:
2. The sly old _____ ran by.
Down:
1. He hopped into a _____ .

Word List: tuba you your

Across:
1. How are _____ ?
Down:
1. Is this _____ book?
2. I play a _____ in my school band.

Horizons® Spelling Grade 1

Key for Week 11 Worksheet

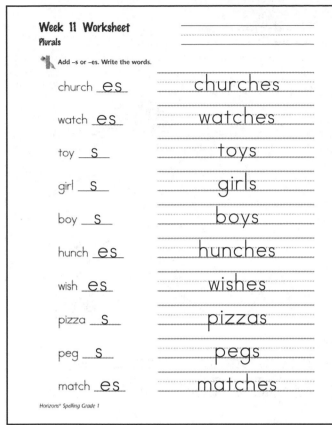

Week 11 Worksheet
Plurals

Add –s or –es. Write the words.

church __es__   churches
watch __es__   watches
toy __s__   toys
girl __s__   girls
boy __s__   boys
hunch __es__   hunches
wish __es__   wishes
pizza __s__   pizzas
peg __s__   pegs
match __es__   matches

Horizons® Spelling Grade 1

Key for Week 12 Worksheet

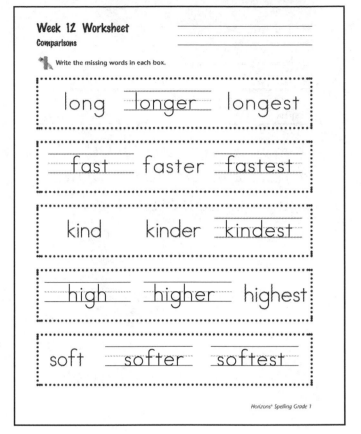

Week 12 Worksheet
Comparisons

Write the missing words in each box.

long __longer__ longest

__fast__ faster __fastest__

kind kinder __kindest__

__high__ __higher__ highest

soft __softer__ __softest__

Horizons® Spelling Grade 1

Key for Week 13 Worksheet

Week 13 Worksheet
Adding –ful, –ing, –ness

Cut and paste the correct suffix beside each word.

fall __ing__   peace __ful__

soft __ness__   snow __ing__

grow __ing__   dark __ness__

cheer __ful__   cook __ing__

joy __ful__   truth __ful__

Horizons® Spelling Grade 1

Key for Week 15 Worksheet

Week 15 Worksheet
oo Sounds

Cut out the word cards at the bottom of the page. Paste them under the correct oo sound.

Book

Moon

Book	Moon
shook	spoon
hook	toot
wood	pool
wool	roof
cook	goose

Horizons® Spelling Grade 1

Key for Week 17 Worksheet

Week 17 Worksheet
Complete the Sentences

Use the words from the word list to complete the sentences.

Word List

our	out	bowl	Paul	house
straw	about	saw	down	yellow

1. Saul's name was changed to __Paul__ .

2. I had soup in a __yellow__ __bowl__ .

3. Did you hear __about__ the party?

4. I __saw__ a big pile of __straw__ at Grandma's farm.

5. I ran __down__ the stairs and __out__ the door.

6. __Our__ car is green.

7. My friend lives in a big white __house__ .

Horizons® Spelling Grade 1

Key for Week 18 Worksheet

Week 18 Worksheet
More Compound Words

Draw lines to connect the words and make compound words. Match the compound words to the pictures.

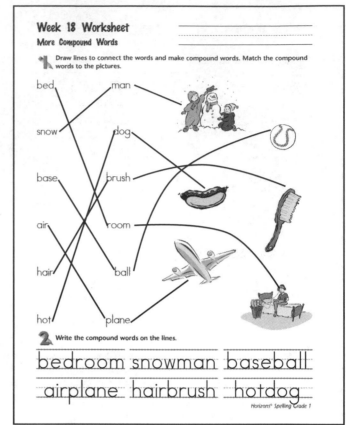

bed — man
snow — dog
base — brush
air — room
hair — ball
hot — plane

2 Write the compound words on the lines.

__bedroom__ __snowman__ __baseball__
__airplane__ __hairbrush__ __hotdog__

Horizons® Spelling Grade 1

Key for Week 22 Worksheet

Week 22 Worksheet
Crossword Fun

Complete the crossword puzzle.

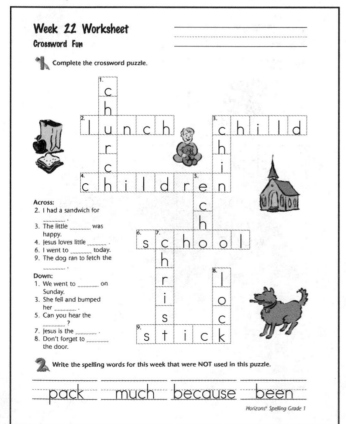

Across:
2. I had a sandwich for _____.
3. The little _____ was happy.
4. Jesus loves little _____.
6. I went to _____ today.
9. The dog ran to fetch the _____.

Down:
1. We went to _____ on Sunday.
3. She fell and bumped her _____.
5. Can you hear the _____?
7. Jesus is the _____.
8. Don't forget to _____ the door.

2 Write the spelling words for this week that were NOT used in this puzzle.

__pack__ __much__ __because__ __been__

Horizons® Spelling Grade 1

Key for Week 23 Worksheet

Week 23 Worksheet
Plurals

Write the plurals of the words.

church __churches__   girl __girls__

watch __watches__   boy __boys__

toy __toys__   hunch __hunches__

2 Choose a word from the word list to complete the sentences.

Word List

who	what	when	where	which	whale

1. __Who__ saw the __whale__ ?

2. __Will__ will you show me __where__ you put the books?

3. __What__ time is it?

4. __Which__ dog is yours?

Horizons® Spelling Grade 1

Key for Week 26 Worksheet

Week 26 Worksheet
More Opposites

🐾 Draw a line to connect the words that are opposites.

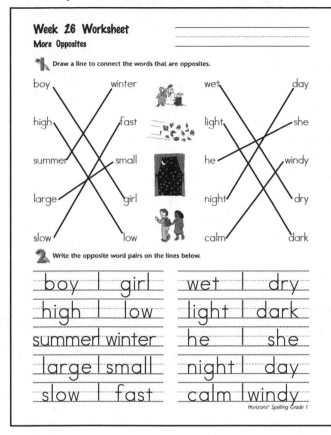

boy — winter
high — fast
summer — small
large — girl
slow — low

wet — day
light — she
he — windy
night — dry
calm — dark

2️⃣ Write the opposite word pairs on the lines below.

boy	girl		wet	dry
high	low		light	dark
summer	winter		he	she
large	small		night	day
slow	fast		calm	windy

Horizons® Spelling Grade 1

Key for Week 27 Worksheet

Week 27 Worksheet
More Homophones

🐾 Complete the sentences by underlining the correct homophone.

1. (Won, <u>One</u>) day, John (<u>won,</u> one) a race.
2. Did you come here to (<u>see</u>, sea) the (<u>see</u>, sea) lions?
3. The wind (blue, <u>blew</u>) Mary's (<u>blue</u>, blew) hat off.
4. (Know, <u>No</u>) (<u>won</u>, one) (<u>knew</u>, new) the answer to the teacher's question.
5. (Eye, <u>I</u>) got some dust in my (<u>eye</u>, I).
6. At what (our, <u>hour</u>) will we be eating (<u>our</u>, hour) meal?
7. Matt looked (<u>pale</u>, pail) when he dropped the (pale, <u>pail</u>) of water.
8. Did you (here, <u>hear</u>) me call you over (<u>here</u>, hear)?
9. Last (<u>night</u>, knight) I read a story about a (night, <u>knight</u>).
10. Bill does (knot, <u>not</u>) (<u>know</u>, no) how to untie the (<u>knot</u>, not) in his shoelace.
11. Please (<u>wait</u>, weight) while I check my (wait, <u>weight</u>) on the scale.
12. (Eye, <u>I</u>) can (<u>see</u>, sea) the (see, <u>sea</u>) from my bedroom window.

Horizons® Spelling Grade 1

Key for Week 29 Worksheet

Week 29 Worksheet
Dictionary Work

🐾 Look up these words in your Spelling Dictionary. Copy the sentence you find there on the first line. Write a new sentence of your own on the second line.

Dictionary: ^{serve} Jesus wants us to serve each other.

My sentence:_____

Dictionary: ^{first} Ellen was the first one in line.

My sentence:_____

Dictionary: ^{shirt} Tom wore his blue shirt to church.

My sentence:_____

Dictionary: ^{behind} Josh was behind Julie in line.

My sentence:_____

Dictionary: ^{over} The cow jumped over the moon.

My sentence:_____

Dictionary: ^{bird} Have you ever seen a bird with red wings?

My sentence:_____

Dictionary: ^{burn} Be careful not to burn yourself on the stove.

My sentence:_____

Dictionary: ^{purple} Judy's face was purple after she ate the grape candy.

My sentence:_____

Horizons® Spelling Grade 1

Key for Week 31 Worksheet

Week 31 Worksheet
Adding the Suffix -ing to Words

RULE: If a word with a short vowel ends in a single consonant, usually double the consonant before adding a suffix that begins with a vowel.

RULE: If a word ends in silent e, drop the e before adding a suffix that begins with a vowel.

🐾 Using your rules for this week, add -ing to the following words. Write the words.

hit + ing = **hitting**   win + ing = **winning**

skip + ing = **skipping**   zip + ing = **zipping**

get + ing = **getting**   mop + ing = **mopping**

pop + ing = **popping**   rub + ing = **rubbing**

2️⃣ Using your rules for this week, add -ing to the following words. Write the words.

rope + ing = **roping**   file + ing = **filing**

come + ing = **coming**   fake + ing = **faking**

love + ing = **loving**   hide + ing = **hiding**

mine + ing = **mining**   wipe + ing = **wiping**

wave + ing = **waving**   ride + ing = **riding**

Horizons® Spelling Grade 1

Reproducible Phonics Rules Flashcards

1. Long vowels say their names.

ā

ē

ī

ō

ū

2. When a word has one vowel, the vowel usually has the short sound.

căt

bĕd

pĭn

cŏt

hŭt

răn

pĕp

dĭg

hŏt

gŭm

3. In words with a vowel, a consonant, and an e at the end, the first vowel sound is long and the e is silent.

mād¢   tīr¢

rāk¢   flūt¢

hōp¢   tūb¢

cōn¢   dīm¢

bīk¢   hīd¢

4. When c or g are followed by e, i, or y, they make the soft sound. When c or g are followed by a, u, o, or a consonant, they make the hard sound.

Soft c	ceiling, city, ice
Hard c	cake, cut, cane
Soft g	gem, giant, giraffe
Hard g	sugar, grape, glass

5. A consonant digraph is two or more consonants that stay together to make their special sound.

Beginning	Ending	
<u>th</u>in	pa<u>th</u>	bri<u>gh</u>t
<u>ch</u>op	mu<u>ch</u>	si<u>gn</u>
<u>sh</u>op	di<u>sh</u>	ca<u>tch</u>
<u>ph</u>one	gra<u>ph</u>	com<u>b</u>
<u>kn</u>ife	dou<u>b</u>t	phle<u>gm</u>
<u>ch</u>orus	Jo<u>hn</u>	
<u>g</u>naw	colu<u>mn</u>	
<u>wh</u>ip	clo<u>ck</u>	
<u>w</u>rite	lau<u>gh</u>	

6. A vowel pair is two vowels that come together to make one long vowel sound. The first vowel is long, and the second vowel is silent.

ā $̸i$ rain, train, paint

ā $̸y$ pray, hay, tray

ē $̸e$ peek, creek, teeth

ē $̸a$ dream, seal, read

ī $̸e$ pie, tie, lie

ō $̸a$ goat, roam, soap

ō $̸e$ doe, hoe, toe

7. A sentence is a complete thought that tells who did what.
   Every sentence starts with a capital letter and ends with a period (.), a question mark (?), or an exclamation mark (!).

Statement (.):

   I am in the first grade.

Question (?):

   What grade are you in?

Exclamation (!):

   Wow! We are in the same grade!

8. A capital letter is used at the beginning of every sentence. Names of people and places begin with a capital letter.

Does Jane like ice cream?

Jim and Jill will take a trip to Texas.

Will Ann and Bob go with them?

Horizons Spelling Grade 1

9. A compound word is made from two or more words joined together to make one word.

mail + box = mailbox

cup + cake = cupcake

dog + house = doghouse

rain + coat = raincoat

pop + corn = popcorn

10. When a word ends in ss, ch, sh, or x, you usually add es at the end to make the word plural.

dress   +   es   =   dresses

church   +   es   =   churches

dish   +   es   =   dishes

fox   +   es   =   foxes

11. When a word ends in a vowel plus y, you usually add s at the end to make the word plural.

turk<u>ey</u>　+　s　=　turkeys

j<u>ay</u>　+　s　=　jays

t<u>oy</u>　+　s　=　toys

monk<u>ey</u>　+　s　=　monkeys

12. When a word ends in f or fe, change the f to a v and add es to make the word plural.

wolf – f + v + es = wolves

leaf – f + v + es = leaves

wife – fe + v + es = wives

calf – f + v + es = calves

13. A suffix is an ending that is added to a base word. Many words do not have to have their spelling changed before a suffix is added.

Base Word	+	Suffix	=	New Word
rain	+	ed	=	rained
lift	+	ing	=	lifting
hope	+	ful	=	hopeful
safe	+	ly	=	safely
care	+	less	=	careless
kind	+	ness	=	kindness
open	+	s	=	opens
trick	+	y	=	tricky

14. The suffix –er is used to compare two things.
The suffix –est is used to compare more than two things.

Suffix –er:

Bill is tall<u>er</u> than Ben and short<u>er</u> than Dan.

Suffix –est:

Dan is the tall<u>est</u> of the three boys.

15. If a word with a short vowel ends in a single consonant, you usually double the consonant before adding a suffix that begins with a vowel.

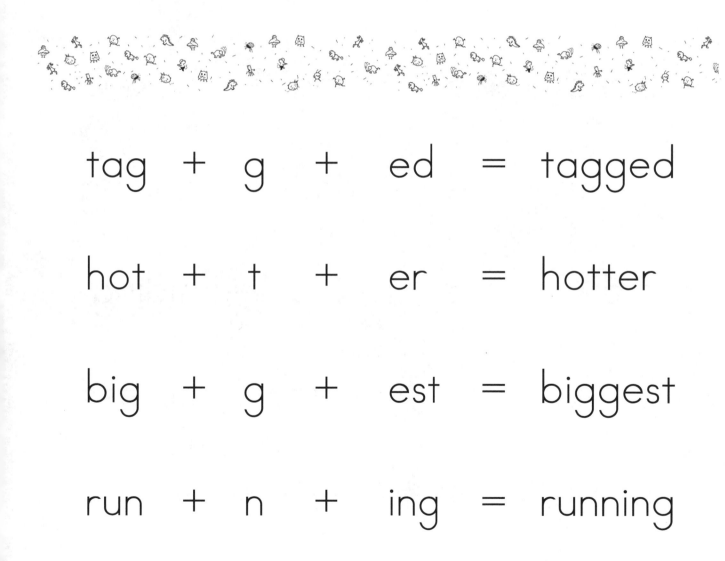

tag + g + ed = tagged

hot + t + er = hotter

big + g + est = biggest

run + n + ing = running

16. If a word ends in silent e, drop the e before adding a suffix that begins in a vowel.

bake   –   e   +   ing   =   baking

shine   –   e   +   ing   =   shining

hide   –   e   +   ing   =   hiding

cute   –   e   +   est   =   cutest

smile   –   e   +   ed   =   smiled

17. When a word ends in a single or a double consonant, the spelling does not usually need to be changed when adding the suffixes −y, −en, or −able.

Base Word + Suffix = New Word

speed	−y	speedy
sharp	−en	sharpen
break	−able	breakable

18. A consonant blend is two or more consonants that work together at the beginning or end of a word. Each consonant says its own sound.

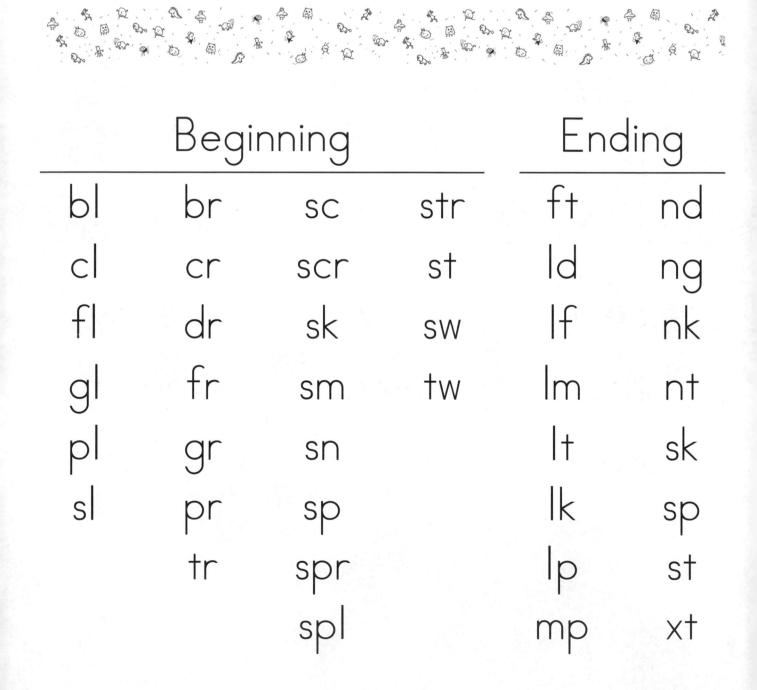

Beginning				Ending	
bl	br	sc	str	ft	nd
cl	cr	scr	st	ld	ng
fl	dr	sk	sw	lf	nk
gl	fr	sm	tw	lm	nt
pl	gr	sn		lt	sk
sl	pr	sp		lk	sp
	tr	spr		lp	st
		spl		mp	xt

19. Vowel digraphs are two vowels put together in a word that make a long or short sound or have a special sound all their own.

aw, au	saw, auto, draw, Paul
ea	head, dread, sweater
ei	eight, weigh, sleigh
ew	few, threw, knew
oo	good, stood, book
oo	pool, school, tool

20. When x comes at the end of a word, it usually is pronounced ks. When it comes at the beginning of a word, it often makes the z sound.

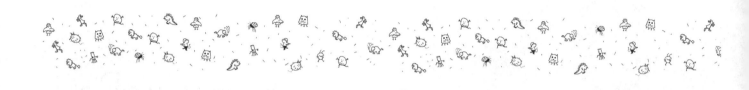

Beginning "z" sound	Ending "ks" sound
xylophone	box
Xerox	fox
	suffix
	prefix

21. When a word ends in y after a consonant, change the y to i before adding –er or –est to the end.

busy – y + er = busier

early – y + est = earliest

happy – y + er = happier

sunny – y + er = sunnier

funny – y + est = funniest

22. A contraction is a word that is made from two words.
Two words are put together, and one or more letters are left out.
An apostrophe (') is used in place of those letters.

cannot   –   no + '   = can't

let us   –   u + '   = let's

it is   –   i + '   = it's

I am   –   a + '   = I'm

you have – ha + '   = you've

we are   –   a + '   = we're

23. In an r—controlled vowel, an r after the vowel makes the vowel sound different from a short or long sound.

ar	farm, park, dark, star
er	clerk, fern, swerve, perch
ir	twirl, shirt, dirt, whirl
or	born, storm, horse, corn
ur	purse, church, purr, surf

24. A vowel diphthong is two vowels that blend together to make one sound.

ow	cow, town, brown, clown
ow	snow, elbow, know, throw
ou	mouth, south, house, round
oi	boil, coin, soil, voice
oy	toy, joy, boy, enjoy

25. Sometimes, y at the end of a word can make the long ē or long ī sound.

Long ē sound

baby

happy

puppy

penny

Long ī sound

fly

cry

try

why

26. Synonyms are words that mean the same or almost the same thing but are spelled differently.

Antonyms are words that are the opposite or almost the opposite in meaning.

Homonyms are words that sound the same but have different spellings and different meanings.

Synonyms	Antonyms	Homonyms
happy/glad	hot/cold	sent/cent
gift/present	light/dark	won/one
unhappy/sad	loose/tight	fair/fare

27. The letters **qu** make the kw sound.

queen

quilt

quarter

question

quit

quite

quiet

quick

28. The letter s can stand for the s, z or sh sounds.

s sound   z sound   sh sound

seam   raise   sure

sign   noise   sugar

sock   please   assure

                 rise

Horizons Spelling Grade 1

Cumulative Word List
Spelling 1

A

a	after	always	and	ate
about	airport	am	are	ax
add	all	an	arm	

B

back	been	black	bowl	brown
ball	begging	bless	box	burn
be	behind	blue	boxes	but
beaches	big	boat	boy	butterfly
because	bird	boil	bread	
bed	birthday	book	brother	

C

calling	cat	Christ	climb	could
came	cent	Christmas	clock	cupful
can	child	church	cold	cute
can't	children	city	come	
car	chin	classes	cough	

D

day	do	don't	dresses
did	does	door	drop
dishes	dolls	down	

E

Easter	echo	eight	eye
eat	eggs	every	

F

farm	find	fly	for	free
faster	first	food	forget	friend
fastest	five	foot	four	frog
feet	fix	football	fox	from

G

gate	gift	gnat	God	great
gentle	girl	go	good	green
get	glass	goat	goodness	

H

handful	haven't	high	hop	house
happiness	he	higher	hope	hugged
happy	head	highest	hoping	hugging
hard	her	his	hopped	
have	hide	home	hopping	

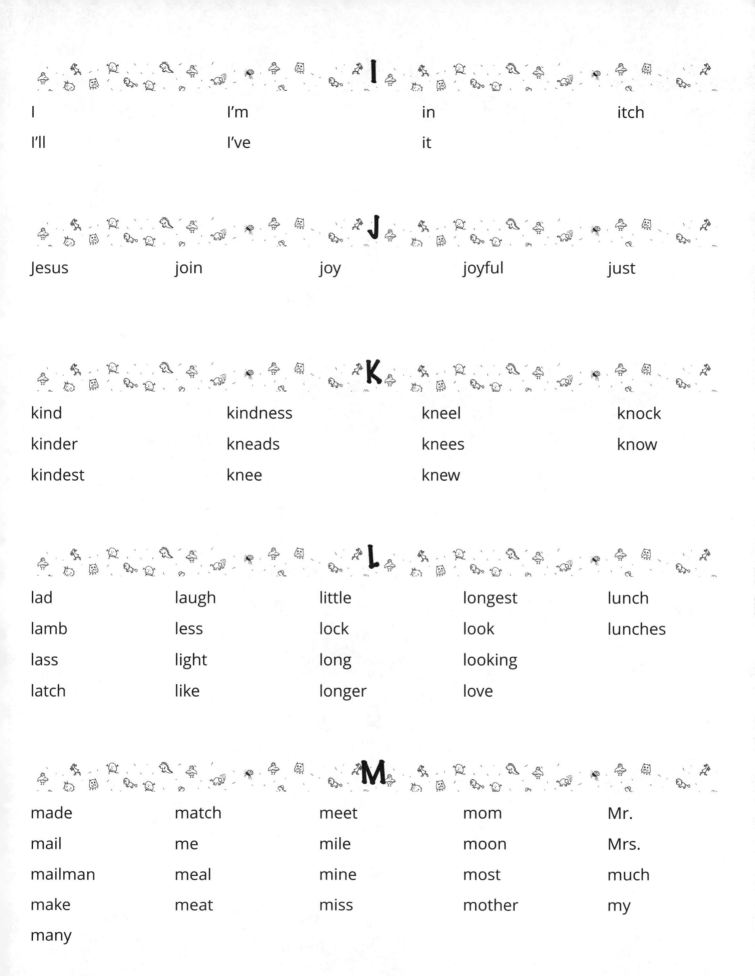

I

I	I'm	in	itch
I'll	I've	it	

J

Jesus	join	joy	joyful	just

K

kind	kindness	kneel	knock
kinder	kneads	knees	know
kindest	knee	knew	

L

lad	laugh	little	longest	lunch
lamb	less	lock	look	lunches
lass	light	long	looking	
latch	like	longer	love	

M

made	match	meet	mom	Mr.
mail	me	mile	moon	Mrs.
mailman	meal	mine	most	much
make	meat	miss	mother	my
many				

N

never	night	noise	now
nice	nine	not	nurse

O

old	one	other	out
on	or	our	over

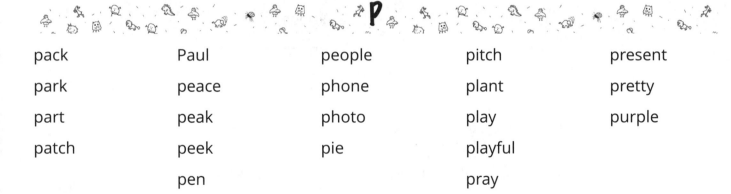

P

pack	Paul	people	pitch	present
park	peace	phone	plant	pretty
part	peak	photo	play	purple
patch	peek	pie	playful	
	pen		pray	

Q

quack	queen	quick	quit

R

rain	right	rode	run
rainbow	road	rough	

S

said	shall	skip	snail	stick
sail	she	skirt	snake	stone
saw	sheep	sky	snow	stop
say	shell	sleep	so	store
school	ship	slip	softer	story
sea	shirt	small	softest	stove
see	shoe	smell	some	straw
serve	short	smiling	something	street
seven	should	smoke	speak	sun
	sign		spelling	

T

tall	then	this	to	tree
ten	there	three	too	trying
thank	they	throw	tooth	tube
that	thick	tie	toss	turn
the	thin	time	tough	two
their	third	toe	toy	

U-V

under	up	use	very
until	us		

W

walk	weak	whale	which	wishes
walls	week	what	white	with
was	well	when	who	write
watch	went	where	whole	
	were		will	

X-Y-Z

x-ray	yellow	you	you're	zoo
yawn	yes	your	zero	